GERMAN 88MM GUN
VS
ALLIED ARMOUR

North Africa 1941–43

DAVID GREENTREE & DAVID CAMPBELL

OSPREY PUBLISHING

Bloomsbury Publishing Plc

PO Box 883, Oxford, OX1 9PL, UK

1385 Broadway, 5th Floor, New York, NY 10018, USA

E-mail: info@ospreypublishing.com

www.ospreypublishing.com

OSPREY is a trademark of Osprey Publishing Ltd

First published in Great Britain in 2021

ISBN: PB 9781472841155; eBook 9781472841162; ePDF 9781472841131; XML 9781472841148

21 22 23 24   10 9 8 7 6 5 4 3 2 1

Artwork by Ian Palmer

Maps by Bounford.com

Index by Zoe Ross

Typeset by PDQ Digital Media Solutions, Bungay, UK

Printed and bound in India by Replika Press Private Ltd.

Osprey Publishing supports the Woodland Trust, the UK's leading woodland conservation charity.

To find out more about our authors and books visit **www.ospreypublishing.com**. Here you will find extracts, author interviews, details of forthcoming events and the option to sign up for our newsletter.

Dedication

To Marius Leier, translator extraordinaire.

Acknowledgements

The authors would like to thank Bernhard Kast of Military History Visualized (https://www.youtube.com/c/MilitaryHistory) for his help in sourcing information on the deployment of FlaK artillery in the ground defence role; Graham Campbell for the cakes; Geoff Banks for his never-ending fraternal melodrama; and Nikolai Bogdanovic for his editorial touch.

Editor's note

For ease of comparison between metric and Imperial units, please refer to the following conversion table:

1yd = 0.9m

1ft = 0.3m

1in = 2.54cm/25.4mm

1 long ton = 1.02 metric tonnes

1lb = 0.45kg

Abbreviations

AA	anti-aircraft
AOK	Armeeoberkommando (Army Higher Command)
AP	armour piercing
APBC	armour-piercing ballistic capped
APCBC	armour-piercing capped ballistic cap
AT	anti-tank
CS	Close Support
DAK	Deutsches Afrika Korps
FMG	Funkmessgerät
GOC	General Officer Commanding
HE	high-explosive
K	Kanonier (gunner)
KG	Kampfgruppe(n)
MG	machine gun
NZ	New Zealand
QF	quick firing
RAC	Royal Armoured Corps
SP	self-propelled
TO&E	Table of Organization and Equipment
VVSS	vertical volute spring suspension
WDF	Western Desert Force

Front cover, above: A German FlaK 18 position. (Ian Palmer)

Front cover, below: 'The Saint' Crusader II from A Squadron, 10th Royal Hussars, 2nd Armoured Brigade, 1st Armoured Division, in Libya 1942. (Ian Palmer)

Key to unit symbols

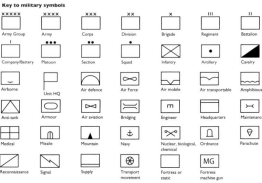

CONTENTS

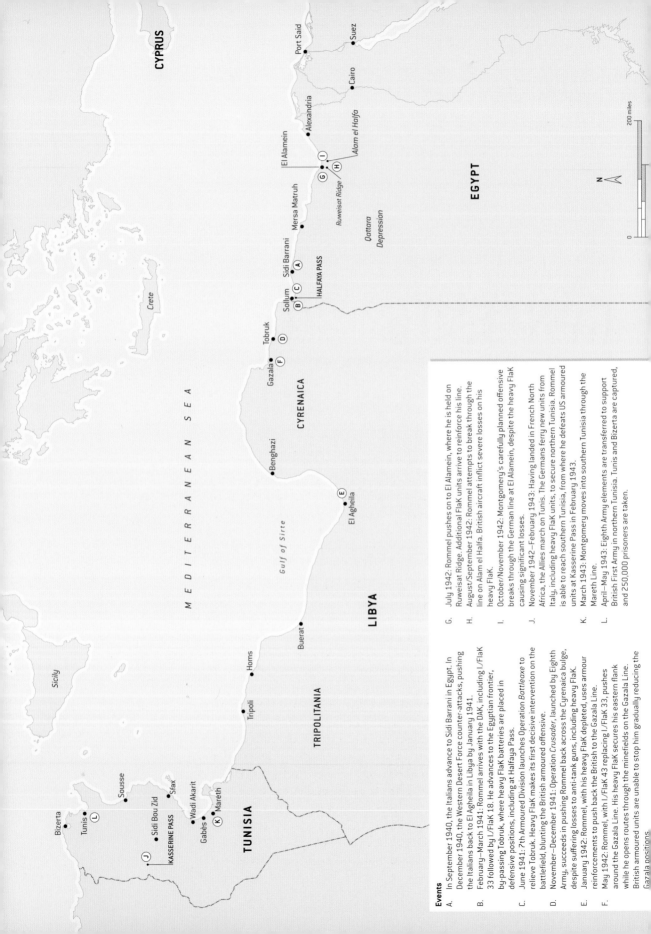

CYPRUS

MEDITERRANEAN SEA

Sicily

Crete

Gulf of Sirte

Port Said
Suez
Cairo
Alexandria
El Alamein
Alam el Halfa
Ruweisat Ridge
Qattara Depression
Mersa Matruh
Sidi Barrani
Sollum
HALFAYA PASS
Tobruk
Gazala
Benghazi
El Agheila
Buerat
Homs
Tripoli

Bizerta
Tunis
Sousse
Sfax
Sidi Bou Zid
KASSERINE PASS
Wadi Akarit
Gabès
Mareth

CYRENAICA
TRIPOLITANIA
LIBYA
TUNISIA
EGYPT

N

0   200 miles

Events

A. In September 1940, the Italians advance to Sidi Barrani in Egypt. In December 1940, the Western Desert Force counter-attacks, pushing the Italians back to El Agheila in Libya by January 1941.

B. February–March 1941: Rommel arrives with the DAK, including I./FlaK 33 followed by I./FlaK 18. He advances to the Egyptian frontier, by-passing Tobruk, where heavy FlaK batteries are placed in defensive positions, including at Halfaya Pass.

C. June 1941: 7th Armoured Division launches Operation *Battleaxe* to relieve Tobruk. Heavy FlaK makes its first decisive intervention on the battlefield, blunting the British armoured offensive.

D. November–December 1941: Operation *Crusader*, launched by Eighth Army, succeeds in pushing Rommel back across the Cyrenaica bulge, despite suffering losses to anti-tank guns, including heavy FlaK.

E. January 1942: Rommel, with his heavy FlaK depleted, uses armour reinforcements to push back the British to the Gazala Line.

F. May 1942: Rommel, with I./FlaK 43 replacing I./FlaK 33, pushes around the Gazala Line. His heavy FlaK secures his eastern flank while he opens routes through the minefields on the Gazala Line. British armoured units are unable to stop him gradually reducing the Gazala positions.

G. July 1942: Rommel pushes on to El Alamein, where he is held on Ruweisat Ridge. Additional FlaK units arrive to reinforce his line.

H. August/September 1942: Rommel attempts to break through the line on Alam el Halfa. British aircraft inflict severe losses on his heavy FlaK.

I. October/November 1942: Montgomery's carefully planned offensive breaks through the German line at El Alamein, despite the heavy FlaK causing significant losses.

J. November 1942–February 1943: Having landed in French North Africa, the Allies march on Tunis. The Germans ferry new units from Italy, including heavy FlaK units, to secure northern Tunisia. Rommel is able to reach southern Tunisia, from where he defeats US armoured units at Kasserine Pass in February 1943.

K. March 1943: Montgomery moves into southern Tunisia through the Mareth Line.

L. April–May 1943: Eighth Army elements are transferred to support British First Army in northern Tunisia. Tunis and Bizerta are captured, and 250,000 prisoners are taken.

INTRODUCTION

The British were keen advocates of armour. In the interwar era J.F.C. Fuller, a general that had utilized armour in World War I, developed ideas about mechanized warfare along with Basil Liddell Hart. Armour would end the immense losses suffered in World War I by bringing mobility back to the battlefield. They wanted armour to operate independently, unfettered by slower infantry and towed guns. Infantry would be used solely to occupy territory. The infantry were not keen on this idea; they had a combined doctrine that envisaged heavy infantry tanks supporting them in the attack whilst lighter tanks would be used in manoeuvre warfare.

In the 1920s the Experimental Mechanised Force had persuaded the General Staff to give tanks an independent operational role; however, though infantry would be separated at brigade level because trucks could not accompany tanks on the battlefield, infantry would be committed to some operations with tanks at divisional level. The latest Field Service Regulations prior to the war, stressing how orders needed to be followed in accordance with the master plan, advocated infantry divisions supported by tank battalions of slow-moving heavy infantry tanks breaking the enemy line. The mobile division with faster cruiser tanks would then exploit. Combined arms operations in the desert would be hampered by this different use of armour.

German doctrine sought to utilize tanks as part of combined arms groups and developed existing doctrine that stressed a war of movement. Manoeuvring fast at the operational level had enabled Prussian armies in previous wars to defeat their enemies in detail. A battle of annihilation, termed a Vernichtungsschlacht, was sought through envelopment or encirclement because the German assumption was that their forces would always be inferior to those of their enemies. Making decisions and maintaining a high tempo of operations by both senior and junior leaders leading from the front was stressed through the doctrine of mission command. Senior commanders limited orders

A FlaK 18 in ground battle against French tanks, May 1940. In France in May 1940, six self-propelled FlaK 18 and 33 FlaK 18 with shield were deployed in Panzerjäger-*Abteilungen*. Luftwaffe FlaK-Regiments with FlaK 18 towed by the SdKfz 7 were also deployed in support of ground forces, and the FlaK 18 gained a reputation as the only gun capable of destroying heavy tanks. Rommel deployed it to defeat the Matilda's 78mm frontal armour near Arras, destroying 24 in quick succession. The self-propelled FlaK 18 gun was not in favour, because with the gun mounted on the SdKfz 8, the crew had little room to fire the weapon. Traverse was also limited to 15° either side. Only the six in France were available for the invasion of Russia in 1941, and the last of them was lost in 1943. (Ullstein Bild via Getty Images)

to general objectives and times; junior commanders were given their orders verbally and would immediately decide how to gain the objectives. Aggressive tactics were encouraged to seize the initiative; hesitation was not compatible with the German approach to warfare. In the defence, certain positions could be evacuated when faced with a superior force in order to preserve forces prior to commencing a counterattack.

In the German army, training stressed combined arms tactics, whilst the British did not think this was a priority and favoured tank-heavy divisions. German panzer divisions, the same size in tanks as the British tank brigade, had a full complement of support units; initially the British armoured brigade had none. The British did not realize the limitations of the new armoured technology. Fuller did not see a role for artillery in a fast-paced armoured battle. The role of the tank in British doctrine was to eliminate enemy tanks. The Germans used AT guns, especially heavy 8.8cm FlaK guns, to destroy enemy armoured formations. Tanks would be used to entice enemy armour onto the guns and would seek to avoid combat with enemy tanks. Armoured divisions, rather than seek out enemy armour, would follow the path of least resistance. AT guns, not limited in calibre to what could be fitted onto a turret, had superior guns to tanks and proved lethal at double the range of most guns in turrets. British tanks found detecting emplaced guns difficult; however, when found, they were vulnerable to British infantry and guns firing HE (high-explosive) shells. Initially the British had a paucity of armour that had HE rounds and had to rely on their field guns.

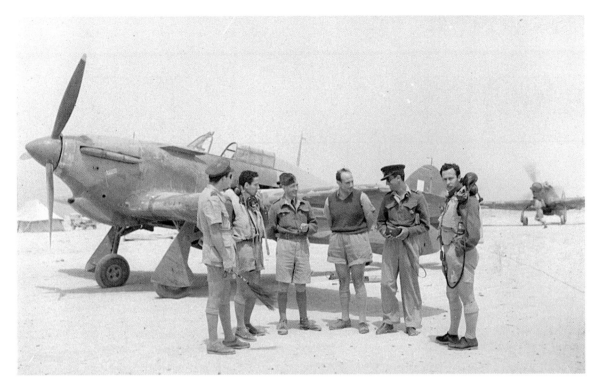

Armour was seen by the British as the weapon that would win the 1940–43 Desert War in North Africa, because the terrain did not limit their movement in the same way as it did in France in 1940. In the desert the influence of armour was emphasized because the use of terrain to enhance defensive positions was limited. In Egypt the desert was flat with hard sand and some small lighter sand patches, largely covered with intermittent scrub and entirely covered with small stones; in Libya there were long gentle slopes and sometimes boulders that reduced the tanks to a crawl. Rock-hard or sandy surfaces made entrenchments difficult to build. Infantry relied on mines in order to assist in the development of effective defensive positions. The lack of natural barriers meant both sides had open flanks. Enveloping the enemy was nearly always achievable. Lines were not contiguous because there were not enough men to cover the distances involved. Maintaining large armies in the field was not an option. Movement at night across trackless terrain brought forces into play against an isolated enemy defensive position. Dust was used to conceal the approach and deceive the enemy as to what was where. Static units had to maintain all-round defensive positions and were some distance apart; for example, the brigade boxes on the Gazala Line in May 1942 were not mutually supporting, did not have their trucks and were not mobile. If British units lost their armour, the fear was that their infantry would be exposed to enemy armour without tank support and suffer crippling losses. Armour needed to be kept close by in order to counter German armoured *Kampfgruppen* and thus was not available to the same extent as German armour to exploit breakthroughs. German AT guns, with British armoured units dispersed to protect the infantry, would encounter enemy tanks committed against them in brigade- rather than divisional-sized units.

Pilots of No. 335 (Hellenic) Squadron RAF in front of a Hawker Hurricane Mark I at LG 20/ Qotafiyah I, west of Daba, Egypt, April 1942. During Operation *Battleaxe*, close air support would be on average three hours away from when forward controllers at brigade HQ requested it. During Operation *Crusader*, close air support on average took two hours because of the need to find fighter escort. In May 1942 response time was lowered further. Close air support was still rare because of the risk of targeting friendly forces. Fighter-bombers flew from May 1942 and targeted enemy guns, including heavy FlaK. (Cecil Beaton/ Imperial War Museums via Getty Images)

CHRONOLOGY

1940

September   The Italians advance to Sidi Barrani in Egypt.

December   Western Desert Force (WDF) attacks, pushing the Italians back to El Agheila in Libya by January 1941.

1941

February   Rommel arrives with the DAK, including I./FlaK 33.

March   Rommel advances to the Egyptian frontier, bypassing Tobruk; heavy FlaK batteries are placed in defensive positions on the border.

June   7th Armoured Division launches Operation *Battleaxe* to relieve Tobruk. Heavy FlaK of I./FlaK 33 at point 208 and Halfaya Pass especially causes severe losses to British armour units.

October   22nd Armoured Brigade of the inexperienced 1st Armoured Division reinforces Eighth Army.

November   6. and 8./FlaK 25, having safely disembarked in the summer, are brought to Tobruk. The British have 738 tanks, including 25 light tanks, 339 Cruisers, 173 Stuarts and 201 Infantry tanks with an operational reserve of 259 (including 90 light); the Germans 390 tanks, including 146 Italian. The 7th Armoured Division has 7th, 22nd and 4th Armoured brigades.

November–December   Operation *Crusader* launched by Eighth Army succeeds in pushing Rommel back across the Cyrenaica bulge, despite suffering losses to German AT guns including heavy FlaK.

1942

January   Rommel, his heavy FlaK depleted, has armour reinforcements that push back the newly arrived 2nd Armoured Brigade; Eighth Army pulls back to the Gazala Line.

April   I./FlaK 43 replaces I./FlaK 33. I./FlaK 6 is also disembarked. Grants and 6-pdr AT guns arrive to equip the British armoured units.

27 May   Rommel pushes around the Gazala Line with the DAK. The I./FlaK 43 defeats 4th Armoured Brigade.

28 May   A Squadron, 10th Hussars of 2nd Armoured Brigade with Crusaders is nearly destroyed by heavy fire from 3./FlaK 43.

Early June   Rommel clears a way through the minefields. British armoured units are unable to stop him gradually reducing the Gazala positions.

1 July   Though nearly 1,200 British tanks were knocked out during the Gazala battles, the British have 137 tanks at the front with 42 in transit from workshops. The Axis has 70. Rommel pushes on to El Alamein in Egypt where he is held on Ruweisat Ridge. Additional FlaK units arrive to reinforce his line.

Late August–early September

Rommel attempts to break through the line on Alam el Halfa Ridge. British aircraft cause severe losses to the heavy FlaK.

September

British armoured regiments in 1st and 7th Armoured divisions are given Crusader IIIs and Shermans, equipped with 6-pdr and 75mm guns, respectively. In addition, General Montgomery has 10th Armoured Division in the line.

October–November

Montgomery's offensive breaks through the German line at El Alamein, despite the heavy FlaK causing significant losses.

8 November

US, Free French and British divisions land in French North Africa.

November–December

The Germans ferry new formations from Italy to secure northern Tunisia, including heavy units. Von Arnim's 5.Panzer-Armee is established.

1943

February

Rommel, having reached southern Tunisia, is able to defeat US armoured units at Kasserine Pass.

Late March

Montgomery moves into southern Tunisia through the Mareth Line.

April

Eighth Army elements including 1st Armoured and the new 6th Armoured divisions are transferred to support First Army in northern Tunisia.

23 April

The final offensive by Eighth and First armies begins.

12 May

Tunis and Bizerta are captured, along with 250,000 prisoners.

A column of Matilda II heavy infantry tanks moving 'line ahead' across the desert near Tobruk, 1941. The weapons that the British adopted were best suited to colonial operations rather than a European war. The exception was the infantry tank. In 1940 the needs of the army meant that mass production rather than best possible weapons were prioritized. Of 220 tanks in the *Battleaxe* operation in June 1941, 92 were Matildas of 4th Armoured Brigade, the rest being Cruisers and Crusaders of 7th Armoured Brigade and light tanks of reconnaissance units. (The LIFE Picture Collection via Getty Images)

American M3 Grant tanks in British service, sometime in 1942. Note the ad-hoc camouflage pattern applied to the farther vehicle, something that could depend on the whims of the squadron, troop or individual tank commander. On 27 May, 22nd Armoured Brigade was ordered south to join 4th Armoured Brigade, and was defeated in detail; however, whilst crossing the Trigh Capuzzo, the panzers were severely pummelled by 2nd Armoured Brigade and First Army Tank Brigade. The 90.Leichte-Division was similarly severely treated by 4th Armoured Brigade. Rommel's DAK Kampfstaffel defeated 4th Armoured Brigade only with the support of three batteries of heavy FlaK. (Bob Landry/The LIFE Picture Collection via Getty Images)

DESIGN AND DEVELOPMENT

BRITISH

The doctrine behind infantry and cruiser tanks originated in Plan 1919, the projected late-World War I tank offensive that would have relied on heavy (but slow) Mark V tanks to make the initial breakthrough and then utilize the new lighter and faster tanks such as the Medium Mark A 'Whippet' and Medium Mark B to exploit that breakthrough. This concept was further developed throughout the British Army's experiments with combined arms mechanization in the 1920s and early 1930s, where there was still a belief that it would prove necessary to have a slower and much better-protected tank to spearhead the infantry attack on what were assumed to be World War I-style defensive trench systems. The light and cruiser tanks that were expected to drive through the breaches in the enemy line were conceived as tools of disruption, attacking enemy reserves, lines of

Troops from the Scots Guards advance in tandem with Matilda II infantry tanks in Libya, July 1942. Cooperation between senior infantry commanders and their armoured colleagues was problematic. Lumsden, the commander of 1st Armoured Division, was forced to use infantry of 10th Indian Brigade in a night attack on 4/5 June on the German guns during the Battle of Gazala. Poor reconnaissance had failed to locate the gun positions or notice their withdrawal that evening. The 22nd Armoured Brigade refused to charge in daylight. The infantry criticized them. The Indian infantry positions were attacked that day and the tanks refused to support them, as the divisional commander told them they had no business doing this. (Mirrorpix via Getty Images)

communication and command elements; initially, they were not envisaged as a weapon system with which to seek out and engage other tanks – that was assumed to be under the purview of AT rifles and guns.

There was a lack of a General Staff specification in the prewar years that was indicative of the overall lack of focus that bedevilled the pragmatic aspects of tank design. This problem was exacerbated by the 'shelving' of a number of officers with experience in tank design through the late 1930s, resulting in a loss of institutional knowledge in a critical period. The driving force behind many of the tanks designed in the 1930s were boards made up primarily of industrialists from the firms responsible for their manufacture, an undoubted benefit in understanding the realities of production that would need to be addressed, but they lacked the informed knowledge of what the vehicles were really required to do.

The design and development of tanks and their main armament was divided between the Directorate of Mechanisation and the Royal Artillery, the former looking after the vehicles and the latter the guns that those vehicles would employ. As such there was a disconnect between the two bodies on both technical and doctrinal matters. The army lacked an established technical cadre with experience in tank design and the capability to assist with the nurturing and development of armoured vehicles. There was also no experimental workshop to assist in the evaluation and evolution of tank designs once they had moved from paper to prototype. The practical feedback that would most likely have resulted from such an active engagement by the army was therefore lacking, allowing blind spots to remain and unsuitable or inadequate elements of the design to continue unamended.

There was a belief that speed was more important than armour to a tank's survivability on the battlefield, which encouraged the development of vehicles that were light, but which also lacked the 'upgradeability' found in the more robust and

A12 INFANTRY TANK MARK II (MATILDA), JUNE 1941

This is 'Drake' from No. 1 Troop, A Squadron, 4th Battalion Royal Tank Regiment, 4th Armoured Brigade, 7th Armoured Division, Libya, June 1941. The camouflage scheme followed that devised by Colonel Caunter of the 4th Armoured Brigade, in use from 1940 until October 1941. The base paint layer was BSC. No.61 Light Stone, with the geometric layers being made up of BSC. No.28 Silver Grey and BSC. No.34 Slate. Note the RAC red/white/red recognition markings on both track guards; it was common practice to also apply them to either one or both sides of the turret in a variety of positions and sizes. The war department number 'T6537' is visible on both sides of the hull and the red pennant marks the vehicle as belonging to the squadron's first troop, the second red pennant being an unofficial mark that Drake is the first tank in the troop.

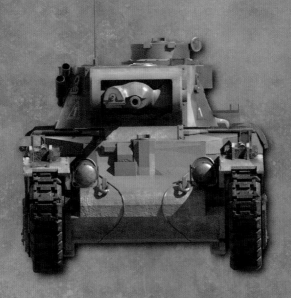

well-balanced German designs. The engines used on pre- and early-war tanks were adaptations and suffered from several weaknesses; no specific tank engine design was developed in time for use in the infantry and cruiser tanks.

The reality of warfare, first in France and then later in North Africa, challenged many of the assumptions that had grown up around the interwar tank formations and their tactical roles, leading to a gradual evolution in doctrine, even though British tank development still continued along the twin tracks of infantry and cruiser vehicles. Added to this, the doctrine prevalent within the 7th Armoured Division had been mostly defined by Major-General Patrick 'Percy' Hobart, GOC of the Mobile Division (Egypt), as the 7th was known before the war. Hobart's ideas, strongly influenced by both Basil Liddell Hart and particularly J.F.C. Fuller, saw the tank as the supreme weapon of the battlefield, dominating terrain and defining the nature of the conflict by its mobility and ability to concentrate at the decisive moment. He paid scant attention to combined arms tactics, and though he was dismissed in 1939, his influence lived on in his division (Moreman 2007, p. 29).

In 1932 the British did not order a replacement tank that could both operate in support of infantry and carry out a wide-ranging operational role. The British by designing the cruiser relied on mobility rather than firepower in order to protect against enemy AT guns; the infantry support design would emphasize armour protection and neglect firepower and mobility. The cruiser tanks were mechanically unreliable though they were fast. Armour on the cruisers was light, and in 1941

A 6-pdr anti-tank gun and its crew, photographed sometime before the Battle of El Alamein, 1942. Although the Ordnance QF 6-pdr (57mm) was ready in early 1941, the decision was made to delay. Either 100 6-pdrs or 600 2-pdrs could be produced, and the latter option was chosen in large part to try to make good some of the losses suffered at Dunkirk. In addition, at the time, the 2-pdr's AP shell was still a capable round that could penetrate most German tank armour at respectable ranges. (The Print Collector/Getty Images)

German 5cm AT guns could knock them out. The Matilda infantry support tank was proof against most German AT guns; however, radius of action was limited to 65km and they were mechanically unreliable. In December 1940, 7th Royal Tank Regiment lost 50 per cent in Libya owing to mechanical breakdown. Prior to Operation *Crusader* 1st Army Tank Brigade decided not to drive its infantry support tanks and this inhibited training. The Valentine infantry support tank was better; however, range was again limited, as was armament.

The light and cruiser tanks, usually equipping traditional cavalry regiments as well as some units of the Royal Tank Regiment, were often employed in the early phase of the North African campaign in much the same fashion as the mounts they had replaced, the Hussar and light dragoon squadrons seeking to use their speed and manoeuvrability to close with the enemy as quickly as possible, overrunning or routing him. After its arrival in the desert the Royal Tank Regiment found that its tactics – a highly mobile advance, ideally on the enemy's flank, firing on the move, until overwhelming him on contact – proved less than satisfactory. The Royal Tank Regiment term for such a headlong charge at the enemy – 'Balaklavering' – proved apt. As the machine gun put paid to horse cavalry tactics in 1914, so the AT gun screen did for its 1941 armoured cruiser equivalent, though it was a lesson that took rather longer to learn than it should have. The infantry tanks, wedded to the doctrine of supporting advancing infantry, found their heavy armour a definite advantage, at least until the arrival of the 8.8cm FlaK batteries, but their low speed and – as time progressed – increasingly poor armament meant that tanks like the Matilda II struggled to adapt to the requirements forced upon it by an enemy with large, manoeuvrable armoured forces and a well-developed system of AT defence.

Tanks lacked sufficient power to have armour bolted on, and faults were not attended to prior to production. They did not have a sufficiently wide chassis to have a large gun set in the turret because until March 1941 they had to fit onto railway carriages. German armour could target British armour equipped with 2-pdr guns effectively from 900m; the British needed to be within less than half that distance. The Germans, with wider-gauged railways, could place 50mm and 75mm guns on their wider Panzer IIIs and IVs, and, unlike the 2-pdr guns on the British cruisers, they could also fire HE shells. British tanks when encountering enemy AT guns could either wait until their artillery neutralized them or charge. The mortars in the few close support tanks operated by the British would not match the 75mm gun in the early version of the Panzer IV. The Stuart tank was reliable; however, a small 37mm gun and range of 65km were limiting factors. The Grant introduced in May 1942 had good armour, and the 75mm sponson-mounted gun in the hull could use HE shells; its armour-piercing (AP) round was better than the 5cm gun on the Panzer III.

Design reflected how the General Staff expected the tanks to be utilized. Prior to 1942, they thought the tank's role was to fight enemy tanks. Experience showed its use was against enemy AT guns, infantry and trucks. Of British tanks knocked out in North Africa, 40 per cent were because of enemy AT guns and 38 per cent because of enemy tanks. As the war progressed, it was recognized that tanks were often called upon to perform roles other than those for which they had been expressly designed, and that competent 'jack-of-all-trades' vehicles like the M3 Grant and M4 Sherman – medium tanks with a good balance of protection, hitting power and speed – gave

8.8CM FLAK 18 AND SDKFZ PRIME MOVER, 3./FLAK-REGIMENT 33, LATE 1941

The distinctive camouflage pattern is based on a photographic example from mid-1941 to mid-1942, and is almost certainly an example of home-grown initiative on the part of the gun's crew or the battery commander.

The FlaK 18 would be joined in theatre by the FlaK 36, FlaK 37 and eventually the FlaK 41. The prime mover for FlaK 18/36/37 was usually an SdKfz 7 that towed the gun and also transported its 11-man crew, whilst the 11,200kg FlaK 41 required the meatier SdKfz 8 Schwerer Zugkraftwagen 12t half-track.

armoured units the flexibility they needed. Their arrival in 1942 gave the armoured brigades vehicles that were more reliable, better armed, and often better protected than those they had been using up to that point. That July, the General Staff had decided to prioritize mechanical reliability, a gun with HE shells, and an operational range of at least 160km. The Sherman that was with some armour units at El Alamein in October 1942 had the 75mm gun in a turret and could engage enemy AT guns from hull-down positions at 2,500m, though German 5cm guns could still knock them out. The Cromwell tank, initially given a 6-pdr, had a 75mm gun fitted. The Churchill was the last infantry support tank and could withstand 50mm AT hits

QF 3.7in. (94mm) guns from an AA battery ready for action in the Western Desert, c.1941. Allied nations would generally not use AA guns on armour, in part because they did not have the inclination, and also because they were not flexible-minded enough to develop the required doctrine. The 3.7in. gun would mainly be used against planes and not against tanks because the weapon relied on range data provided by radar and did not have a dedicated optical sight. Even so, it was expected to be able to fire against ground targets in emergencies, but the gun's design did not readily accommodate prolonged fire at low elevations. In addition, little AP ammunition was provided for the 3.7in., and it was also relatively slow to move and deploy, being two tons heavier than an '88'. (Bettmann/Getty Images)

and operate on steep gradients. In Tunisia tanks would fire only 25 per cent of their ammo against enemy armour.

Prewar designs were deemed suitable for the time, and were equipped with a good 2-pdr gun, but they were hamstrung by a number of factors that were exposed by the pressures of war: a lack of an overarching set of design principles for tanks; dislocation between the different bodies responsible for the design, construction, armament and employment of the vehicles; and a lack of technical and institutional knowledge within the army to influence and correct the designs and ensure that they were fit for purpose.

GERMAN

In 1914, when aircraft made a difference on the battlefield, the Germans established units to shoot them out of the sky. Initially field guns were used with extended-length barrels and mountings capable of high elevation. During late 1916 the first 8.8cm gun in this role appeared. This was a development of the standard L/45 naval gun, chosen because a gunner could carry this weight of round (15kg) without mechanical assistance. Krupp and Rheinmetall produced guns termed 8.8cm FlaK 16. The projectile and propellant-carrying cartridge were joined together in order to increase loading speed. The 45-cal. barrel size could fire a 9.6kg HE time-fused shell with a muzzle velocity of 765m/s to a practical height of nearly 7,000m. The mounting on a flat platform on a twin-axled trailer was stabilized in action by folding outriggers on each side.

The Versailles Treaty at the end of World War I banned the gun and limited the Reichswehr to 7.5 and 10.5cm guns. In the late 1920s Krupp worked with Bofors in Sweden to develop a 7.5cm gun and some went to the German navy. The German army thought the gun too light in projectile terms. The Versailles Treaty did allow

A FlaK 18's crew manhandle it into position, c.1942, North Africa. The 8.8cm FlaK 18, with poor cross-country mobility and its large silhouette, coupled with the difficulty in manhandling and camouflaging it, did not at first suggest the gun could be used effectively to combat tanks. In October 1935 a German report that evaluated AT guns made no mention of the gun in this role, though the experiences of Poland and France would lead to a radical re-evaluation of its capabilities against enemy armour. (Ullstein Bild via Getty Images)

10.5cm guns; however, the projectiles were thought to be too bulky for gunners to carry. The Swedish government ended the Bofors/Krupp association in 1930, and by 1932 German designers back in Essen had designed prototypes for an 8.8cm gun that could fire on targets at 8,000m. By the end of 1933, with the Nazi Party in power, the first models were with the Wehrmacht with designation 8.8cm FlaK 18, suggesting that the design did not flout the Versailles Treaty.

Once the firing platform was lowered from a two-axled carriage, the Sd. Ah. 201 or 202, the barrel could traverse a full 360° either way, stabilized further by lowering two side arms. A trained crew could fire 20rpm; 15rpm were more practical. When the gun fired, the spent cartridge was automatically ejected; the next round could be loaded manually or by a power-assisted rammer. The gun could be brought from its carriage and be ready to fire in 2m 30s. The gun was aimed with a FlaK-Zielfernrohr 20 that had four-power magnification and 17.5° field of view (308m wide at 1,000m range). The range drum was divided into 1/16 increments. The FlaK-Zielfernrohr 20 E range drum was graduated to 9,400m in 100m increments. A range table needed to be used if the newer range drum was not fitted in order to work out the range setting. A Rundblickfernrohr 32 (RblF 32) sight mounted on a bracket on the recuperator cylinder was used in the indirect fire role to determine the adjustment needed to elevation.

The Sonderkraftfahrzeug 7 (SdKfz 7) or special-purpose motorized vehicle towed the gun. A semi-tracked vehicle with wheels on the front axle, this specially designed artillery tractor had a 133hp Maybach engine that could travel 50km/h on roads and 250km on a full tank of petrol on roads or 120km off road. Expensive to build, they were in short supply as they were also employed to tow 15cm artillery guns.

The FlaK 18 initially had a monobloc barrel with service life of 900 rounds. Rheinmetall proposed the Rohr Aufbau 9 (RA 9) barrel comprising a half-length outer jacket, a half-length inner sleeve and three-piece inner tube; the second section of the

A pair of FlaK 18s towed by SdKfz 7s through the centre of Vienna in celebration of the Anschluss, Austria 1938. In 1928 provision was made for a motorized gun on a trailer towed by a motor vehicle. A 10kg shell needed to be propelled at speeds of 850m/s by a gun capable of traversing 360°, elevating at 6° per second and traversing at 8° per second. The trailer, mounted on four tyres, needed to be capable of being towed at speeds of 30km/h. Krupp began working on designs in 1930 on what was named the 8.8cm FlaK 18. In 1932 the Heer stipulated the gun should be capable of being hand-cranked at 2° per second and traversed at 3.6° per second. (London Express/Hulton Archive/Getty Images)

inner tube that experienced the most wear (at the point where the rifling commenced) could be changed in the field by the crew or technicians. In order to limit wear, the rifling here was slightly reduced. With the RA 9, whole barrels did not need to be stockpiled to replace old barrels, only the centre inner tube. These different components of the RA 9 were harder to produce, and because the barrel was heavier the recoil mechanism had to be changed. Experience led to the introduction of two-section inner tubes, because gas leakage and debris were making the joints wear quickly. The inner tube joint was prone to temperature expansion differences with the front end of the shell case; the thin cartridge case expanded and resulted in the case not ejecting properly. The new barrel was used with the FlaK 36, identified by a collar two-thirds along the barrel; the FlaK 18 had a smooth tapering profiled barrel.

The multi-section barrel was not needed later in the war when new propellants like Diglycol and Gudol that burned at lower temperatures were available. Also, iron rather than copper driving bands were introduced that produced less wear. Barrel life was 6,000 and sometimes 10,000 rounds. Later in the war the monobloc was used again; change was slow because production lines could not be reorganized without disrupting production. The RA 9 needed precision engineering to make and debris was able to interfere with the workings of the joints. The RA 9 and two-section inner tube could be used on FlaK 18, 36 and 37. The FlaK 37 was basically the same as the FlaK 36 with changes made to aerial fire control.

The FlaK 41 was produced in time for the Tunisian campaign in late 1942 and early 1943, and 44 were sent; however, only 22 arrived, with the others sunk en route. The gun was much improved, though the mechanics were complicated and workshops would be busy keeping them in the field. The gun had a lower silhouette than other models. The longer gun barrel could be moved back to improve stability during long moves. The round, from the loading tray, was power-loaded by a hydro-pneumatic recuperator gear. This mechanism pushed the round onto rotating rollers that nudged it into the chamber. The larger propellant ammunition loads created intense chamber pressures that led to the cartridge case walls expanding to an extent that was unforeseen when brass shells were used during trials. The shortage of copper led the brass casings to be discontinued when the gun was mass-produced. Difficulties extracting the cases led to blockages; some cases split. Crews were advised to allow the barrel to cool down after 20–25 firings; however, this was not usually practical in combat scenarios. In total 152 guns had the three-section inner tube and painted with a yellow band around the barrel to show they could fire only brass cartridge cased rounds; 133 guns had two-section barrels to alleviate the problem; however, the issue persisted and 271 guns

had a heavier two-piece barrel with a jacket and no sleeve. The SdKfz 8 was used to tow the gun.

The FlaK 18's carriage, the Sd. Ah. 201, had a single set of wheels on the front bogie and two sets of wheels on the rear bogie. The gun would not be pointed in the direction of travel when being towed to reduce wear. By 1939 the Sd. Ah. 202 with each wheel section having two wheels was introduced, meaning the wheels were interchangeable and the gun could be towed with the gun pointing either way. The ride on rough terrain was smoother and the gun could be used whilst still limbered to meet immediate threats. The Sd. Ah. 202 was retrofitted on the FlaK 18 even though the total weight increased from 7,000kg to 8,200kg.

The gun was mounted on a cradle resting on curved trunnions on a conical pedestal. The pedestal was secured on the platform with swinging outrigger arms lowered to the ground in action. Prolonged firing needed the platform to be lowered from the wheels and locked in place with bolts located close to the outriggers. Levelling was done using screw jacks at the end of the outriggers and final fine levelling at the pedestal. In action the barrel was held in place by two equilibrators in cylinders under the trunnions. The gun was elevated and traversed by two wheels on the right-hand side of the barrel. An indicator above the traverse wheel told the gunner where he was in the rotation. A clutch to disengage the elevation mechanism from the curved, toothed elevating rack was disengaged during travel to protect the rack from movement shocks. Whilst in combat, the traversing wheels could be disconnected to permit large changes to be made by the crew pulling or pushing the carriage around.

A FlaK 18 photographed at Bir Hacheim on 4 June 1942. The 10mm-thick *Schutzschild* on the FlaK 18/36/37 provided good protection for the crew servicing the gun. British tanks armed with .303 Vickers or co-axial 7.92mm Besa machine guns were issued only with soft ball ammunition that could not penetrate the FlaK's plate (Jentz 1998, p. 47). Additional protection could be provided in the form of the *Zwischenschild*, a 25cm-wide armoured plate that was fixed in position over the gun's recuperator tube. The gun could be towed with the *Schutzschild* on; however, the *Zwischenschild* needed to be removed before transit. (Bundesarchiv, BA 101I-443-1574-24)

The round for the gun was a combined projectile and shell case. The case was 568mm long and tubular lengths of Diglycol or Gudol propellant were held inside the case with a nitrocellulose igniter. The chemical content was revised in hot-weather regions like North Africa to cater for higher ambient temperatures, and 'Tropen' or 'Tp' to denote tropical was written on the case. HE projectiles were painted yellow with black stencilled markings and were known as the 8.8cm Sprenggranate Patrone (Sprgr. Patr.) L/4.5. The later Sprgr. Patr. 39 and its derivatives were nearly identical except for the dimensions. Early projectiles used copper drive bands; by 1940 less costly and less abrasive sintered iron was used that had FES stencilled on. Explosive filling was 860kg of either TNT/Wax or poured Amatol. The fuse used on ground targets was either percussion or timed, with the latter capable of airbursting. An HE projectile weighed 9.44kg; the complete round was 932mm long and weighed 14.4kg. The 8.8cm guns could be used in an indirect fire role with time-fused HE projectiles. The time fuse needed to be set with a key.

AP rounds used 2.42kg of propellant. The projectile was painted black with red stencilling. The base round was the 8.8cm Panzergranate Patrone (Pzgr. Patr.), a kinetic energy round to go through armour. A softer metal penetrator cap to create streamlining was added to the projectile's cap; this was called Armour-Piercing Capped Ballistic Cap (APCBC) in British intelligence reports. A small TNT/Wax or PETN/Wax charge in the base of the projectile was ignited by a percussion fuse that used a tracer element in order to explode once the projectile had punched through armour and show the gunner where the hit had occurred. The time of 1,000m of flight was 1.25 seconds. Whereas the 8.8cm Pzgr. Patr. had two copper drive bands, on the 8.8cm Pzgr. Patr. 39 and 8.8cm Pzgr. Patr. 39-1 the drive bands were changed to sintered iron. The 8.8cm Pzgr. Patr. 40 rounds had a smaller-calibre penetrator slug machined from tungsten carbide with a tracer element in the base. There was no bursting charge. The higher velocity of the smaller slug created more energy and power at ranges below 1,000m. At half this range another 16mm of armour (in total 126mm) could be punched through. Above this range the improvement was negligible because air resistance lowered the muzzle velocity. Germany did not have access to many mines producing materials used in the production of tungsten carbide and the rounds were in short supply. AP 40 ammunition production ceased altogether in 1943 and rounds were kept for use in critical situations. The 8.8cm Granate Patrone 39 Hohlladung FlaK L/4.7 (Gr. Patr 39 Hl) round used the hollow charge principle. A chemical reaction was produced by Cyclonite/Wax (RDX/Wax) on a thin metal inverted cone when the projectile hit, creating a high temperature jet to burn through metal or concrete. As the 8.8cm gun was rifled, the projectile spin dissipated the centrifugal forces used to create the jet and this made the round unpopular with crews. The cartridge case of the ammunition the FlaK 41 fired was longer in order to accommodate 5.12kg of Gudol propellant, to increase muzzle velocity to 1,000m/s when firing a Sprgr. Gran. 39 HE projectile. The 8.8cm Pzgr. Patr. 39-1 FlaK 41 (muzzle velocity 980m/s) and Pzgr. Patr. 40 FlaK 41 (muzzle velocity 1,025m/s) used 5.42kg of Gudol.

GERMAN AMMUNITION

1. **8.8cm Sprenggranate Patrone 39**. It contained 860g of explosive and when used in the ground role was often equipped with an Az 23/28 (Aufschlagzünder) that had the option of detonation on impact or after a 0.1-second delay. The roman numeral 'IV' denoted the weight classification of the shell ('III' was standard, whereas weight class 'IV' required an adjustment of the firing tables).

2. **8.8cm Panzergranate Patrone 39**. The Pzgr. Patr. 39 contained a small charge of explosive (156g) and included an AP cap to aid in penetration of enemy plate. The explosive charge could be set to explode on impact or after a very brief delay, resulting in detonation within the enemy vehicle. From early 1943 onwards the tips of AP rounds were painted white to aid with loading in low light or darkness.

3. **8.8cm Panzergranate Patrone 40**. It contained a sub-calibre tungsten carbide penetrator slug that contained a tracer element in its base. The slug's effectiveness diminished beyond 500m ranges. Growing shortages of tungsten meant that by 1943 the Pzgr. Patr. 40 was rarely issued.

4. **8.8cm Sprenggranate 39 Patrone FlaK 41**.

5. **8.8cm Panzergranate 39 Patrone FlaK 41**. Though the larger 88×851R mm cartridge cases generated greater muzzle velocity than the 88×571R mm cases used by FlaK 18/36/37 guns, the projectiles were the same.

A British cruiser Mk VI Crusader making the most of its speed, Libya 1942. At 0600hrs on 18 November Operation *Crusader* began. The 22nd Armoured Brigade covered 120km with no sign of the enemy. The next day Italian tanks at Bir el Gobi reduced 2nd Royal Gloucestershire Hussars to a single squadron. On 20 November, 22nd Armoured Brigade moved to Gabr Saleh, where the 4th and 7th Armoured brigades were being roughly handled by German armour. The 22nd Armoured Brigade, with only 17 tanks operational, was at Sidi Rezegh by 22 November. Six tanks of 2nd Royal Gloucestershire Hussars escaped the Battle of Sidi Rezegh on 23 November. Dismounted crews started back to the wire. The unit's armour was wiped out within a week. New tanks would be rapidly found. (Ullstein Bild via Getty Images)

TECHNICAL SPECIFICATIONS

BRITISH

The loss of armour at Dunkirk and the subsequent pressure of defending the home front as well as prosecuting the North African campaign forced the British to make do with what they had, adapting models where possible, rather than undertaking any more substantial redevelopment of their tank arm. The early stages of the war in the desert saw extensive use of early model cruisers and Vickers light tanks, but by mid-1941 their numbers were dwindling. The A15 Cruisers Mk VI and VIA (the Crusader I and II) would replace the worn-out remains of the A13 Mk IIIs and IVs by the end of the year, though some of the older tanks were still in the line during the battles at Sidi Rezegh in November. The losses in Operation *Crusader* were partly

made good by more Crusaders as well as early versions of the Valentine infantry tank and an influx of the new American-made M3 medium tanks known as the 'Grant' in British service (the name 'Lee' was applied to versions of the M3 that used the US-style turret with its additional .30-cal. machine gun). Further disastrous losses during the Battle of Gazala necessitated the emergency rebuilding of the British armoured force yet again, so on 15 July 1942 the US shipped 212 M4A1 and 90 M4A2 Shermans to the British in North Africa (nearly the entire production at the time, something that would have ramifications for the US 1st Armored Division's operations in Tunisia in early 1943). By the time of the Tunisian campaign the British armoured force was largely made up of 6-pdr Crusaders, Valentines and Churchills, as well as significant numbers of M3 Grants and M4 Shermans.

ARMAMENT

The main armament of British cruiser and infantry tanks was a 2-pdr (40mm) gun. The Royal Ordnance QF 2-pdr Mk IX was a fine gun when first introduced, and even by the standards of 1941 it was effective in use against the Panzer III, but developments in armour would see its value gradually diminish. In armoured service it used armour-piercing ammunition exclusively, even though there was an HE shell available.

The 57mm Royal Ordnance QF 6-pdr 7cwt L/43 Mk III was supposed to replace the 2-pdr by 1941 but the vast losses of 2-pdrs incurred at Dunkirk (over 800 AT guns were abandoned) forced the British into an invidious choice: manufacture the 6-pdr even though it was in only the early stages of production and would take time to appear in any significant numbers, or continue with the production of the 2-pdr and plug the gap in AT guns and tank armament with an obsolescent weapon. In addition there was still work to do in adapting existing British tank designs to accommodate the larger gun, with the turret rings of most models like the Matilda II hamstrung by simply being too small to allow for the necessary increase in turret size required by the 6-pdr.

A British-operated M3 Grant with three of its six crew visible, operating in the Western Desert, 1942. Note the counterweight at the end of the barrel on the sponson-mounted M2 75mm gun. Losses during Operation *Crusader* to 2nd Royal Gloucestershire Hussars were 22 officers killed, wounded and missing, and 113 other ranks killed, wounded and missing, with 34 sick. In Egypt in April 1942, they were given Crusaders for G and H squadrons, and Grants for F Squadron. With the Grant, the second in command of the squadron would range his gun on target and then give the range out by wireless. (AirSeaLand Photos, 1000281)

ALLIED AMMUNITION

1. **37mm M51 APC-T.** Used by the M5/M6 guns in the M3 Stuart light tank as well as the M3 Grant's turret.
2. **37mm M74 AP-T.** Quicker and easier to produce than the capped round, it was described as 'effective against homogeneous armor plate, but is likely to ricochet or be deflected on impact with face-hardened armor plate' (TM 9-1904 1944, p. 351).
3. **2-pdr (40mm) AP-T Mk I.** Used in the Royal Ordnance QF 2-pdr Mk IX gun that equipped the Matilda II, Crusader II and Valentine II to V. Penetration of 53mm of armour plate at 60° at 450m was achieved.
4. **6-pdr (57mm) AP Mk 7.** Used in the 57mm Royal Ordnance QF 6-pdr 7cwt L/43 Mk III and the 57mm Royal Ordnance QF 6-pdr 7cwt L/50 Mk V guns, fitted to the Crusader III, Valentine IX, Valentine X and Churchill.
5. **6-pdr (57mm) APCBC Mk 9T.** This round entered service in January 1943, superseding the APC Mk 8T.
6. **75mm M48 HE.** This finally gave British armoured units the chance to take on German anti-tank defences without recourse to field artillery. The standard bursting charge was 680g of TNT in a forged steel warhead with a choice of fuses (the SQ or PD) that gave the option of either a 0.05- or 0.15-second delay respectively.
7. **75mm M72 AP.** Used by the M2/M3 75mm guns in the M3 Grant and M4 Sherman. It was a simplified version of the M61, lacking a bursting charge or a ballistic cap. The M72 was to be used only with a 'SUPER' propelling charge, the increased muzzle velocity being a necessary factor in the penetration of armour plate.
8. **75mm M61 APCBC/HE-T.** The M61 carried a 68g explosive charge, and was to be used only with a 'SUPER' propelling charge. In British service the 75mm rounds were painted black, but with the white band and red central stripe that denoted armour-piercing ammunition.

The Crusader I and II were equipped with a separate machine-gun turret on the front left-hand side of the hull; it was hand-traversed through a 150° arc and mounted a 7.92 x 57mm Besa machine gun, but it was more of a nuisance than a benefit and was often removed in the field, finally being omitted entirely from the Mk III. The Crusader Mk III's 6-pdr gun was an excellent weapon, but production was slow, with carriage-mounted AT guns taking priority – by El Alamein in October 1942 only 100 Crusader Mk III tanks were available (as well as a special tank squadron of six Churchill Mk IIIs in theatre for operational experience; more Churchills would arrive in time for the campaign in Tunisia in January 1943). The gun's larger size forced the Crusader, previously a five-man tank, down to just three, with a predictable impact on the crew's ability to fight the vehicle.

The early A9 and A10 Cruisers had CS or 'Close Support' versions equipped with a 3.7in. howitzer as their main armament, carrying 40 rounds of smoke and a small number of HE shells, though the later A13 Mks I and II did not have HE shells (Fletcher 2017, p. 55). The Matilda II, Crusaders Mk I and Mk II and Valentine III also had CS versions that were equipped with an Ordnance QF 3in. howitzer instead of the 2-pdr gun, a relatively short (25-cal.) weapon that could fire either smoke (6.1kg) or HE (6.3kg) rounds out to an effective range of 1,800m and a maximum range of 2,750m. Usually found only in a squadron's headquarters troop where there would be one or two of the vehicles, the CS tanks were mainly employed in the laying down of smokescreens, with the suppression or destruction of enemy troops and positions using HE shells being seen as a job for the field artillery.

Allied tank main armament				
Gun	Vehicles	Ammunition	Weight (projectile)	Velocity
37mm M5/M6	M3 Stuart/Honey M3 Grant	M74 AP	0.87kg	870m/s (M5) 884m/s (M6)
		M51 APC	0.87kg	
40mm Royal Ordnance QF 2-pdr Mk IX	Matilda II Crusader II Valentine II–V	AP-T, Mk I	1.08kg	792m/s
		APHV-T	1.08kg	853m/s
		APCBC-T, Mk I	2.22kg	792m/s
57mm Royal Ordnance QF 6-pdr 7cwt L/43 Mk III; 57mm Royal Ordnance QF 6-pdr 7cwt L/50 MK V	Crusader III Valentine IX–X Churchill	AP, Mk 7	2.86kg	853m/s (L43) 892m/s (L50)
		APC, Mk 8T	2.86kg	846m/s (L43) 884m/s (L50)
		APCBC, Mk 9T	3.23kg	792m/s (L43) 831m/s (L50)
75mm Gun L/31 M2	M3 Grant	M61 APCBC/HE-T	6.63kg	588m/s
		M72 AP-T	6.32kg	588m/s
75mm Gun L/40 M3	M4 Sherman	M61 APCBC/HE-T	6.63kg	619m/s
		M72 AP-T	6.32kg	619m/s

ENGINES AND SUSPENSION

The American-designed 27L petrol Liberty engines, licensed and built by Nuffield, powered the main British cruiser tanks. The A13 Cruiser Mk III employed a Nuffield Liberty Mk I, and for the A13 Cruiser Mk IV it was a Nuffield Liberty Mk II, whilst the Crusader used a Nuffield Liberty V-12 water-cooled engine (Mks III or IV) that developed 340bhp at 1,500rpm, and which was sited in the front-left section of the vehicle's hull. It used an air-operated Nuffield constant mesh four-speed gearbox and Wilson dual regenerative epicyclic steering, making it fast and responsive, but the Crusader suffered with cooling problems; tank historian David Fletcher noted that the Crusader engine's two cooling fans were 'fitted into the rear engine bulkhead, driven by exposed double roller chains from the crankshaft and geared to turn at double the normal engine speed. In the desert, especially, this caused endless trouble and on later models a form of shaft drive was introduced' (Fletcher 2017, p. 75). It did not help that the air filters were housed on either side of the Crusader's rear deck where they were subject to constant clouds of sand and dust thrown up by the tracks.

The Matilda's powerplant consisted of a pair of 7L AEC 6-cylinder diesels (87hp) or two Leyland cylinder diesels (95hp) that were linked through an epicyclical gearbox, which drove the rear sprockets. For the Valentine, the Mks II, III and VI used an AEC A190 diesel whilst later models (Mks IV, V, VII–XI) used the 6-cylinder GMC 6004 diesel. The Churchill, at around 40 tons, required a Bedford 'flat twelve' 12-cylinder, four-stroke water-cooled, horizontally opposed L-head petrol engine that developed 350hp at 2,000rpm. Both the Matilda and Churchill were grindingly slow, considered an acceptable compromise for their heavy armour and anticipated role as infantry support tanks, though the Churchill would prove to be unusually adept at negotiating steep inclines that would defeat most other vehicles.

The Christie suspension system was first used on the Cruiser Mk III (A13 Mk I) as well as the Cruiser Mk IV (A13 Mk II) and all the subsequent versions of the Crusader, though the Crusaders would utilize five road wheels on each side for better weight distribution, as opposed to the four-a-side design seen on the Mks III and IV tanks. For the infantry tanks the Matilda used the 'Japanese Type' bell crank suspension

M4 Sherman tanks of C Squadron, 9th Queen's Royal Lancers, 2nd Armoured Brigade, 1st Armoured Division, 5 November 1942. On 8 September Shermans arrived in the Western Desert. Their engines were faster and – crucially – easier to maintain. The regiments of 2nd Armoured Brigade had a squadron of 6-pdr Crusader IIIs and two squadrons of 16 Shermans. An indirect-fire technique was developed whereby the tank commander was exposed in the turret with the tank below a crest line, allowing him to observe the fall of shot. The Sherman's high trajectory permitted this type of fire. Moving into and through a minefield in the dark was also practised. (Sgt. Len Chetwyn/ Imperial War Museums via Getty Images)

of five double wheel bogies on each side that had first been developed on the A7. Valentine suspension systems were made of coil springs and hydraulic shock absorbers (by Newton) acting on three wheels at a time (a 'slow motion' system), whilst the Churchill used coil springs to cushion 11 bogies on each side.

For the US-supplied tanks, the M3 Stuart employed a Twin Cadillac Series 42 that developed 220hp at 3,400rpm, and a vertical volute spring suspension (VVSS) system. The M3 (Grant I) had a 340hp Wright (Continental) R975 EC2 engine, the M3A5 (Grant II) a 375hp G.M. 6-71 (dual diesel) engine, both with VVSS systems. The Sherman M4 (Sherman I) and M4A1 (Sherman II) variants used either a Continental R975-C1 or C4 9 cylinder radial gasoline engine that developed 350 or 400hp respectively at 2,400rpm, whilst the M4A2 (Sherman III) used a General Motors 6046 twin inline diesel engine that developed 375hp at 2,100rpm. All three Sherman variants used the same VVSS system.

ARMOUR

The armour thickness on British tanks was developed according to their expected roles, with infantry tanks rather better protected than the fast and nimble cruiser tanks. In the event the requirements that tanks of either type had to fulfil on the actual battlefield often diverged markedly from their expected doctrine, with the lighter armour of the cruisers being a notable shortcoming. The designs on such vehicles usually precluded the addition of any significant protection, and it wasn't until the arrival of the M3 and later M4 medium tanks that the British had something close to decent all-rounders.

Allied tank armour			
Vehicle	Crew	Max. speed km/h	Vehicle
M3 Stuart/Honey	4	58	Turret: 38mm front (50mm gun mantlet), 38mm sides Hull: 38mm front (upper hull), 44mm front (lower hull), 25mm sides
Matilda II	4	24	Turret: 75mm front, side and rear Hull: 78mm front, 55–70mm side, 55mm rear
Crusader I and II[1]	4/5	42	Turret: 40mm front (50mm gun mantlet), 30mm side and rear Hull: 40mm front, 30mm side and rear
Crusader III	3	43	Turret: 40mm front (51mm gun mantlet), 30mm side and rear Hull: 40mm front, 30mm side and rear
Valentine II–V	3/4	24.1	Turret: 65mm front, 60mm sides, 65mm rear Hull: 60mm front, 50–60mm vertical and 30mm sloping sides, 60mm vertical and 17mm sloping rear
Churchill III	5	26	Turret: 89mm front, 76mm side and rear Hull: 102mm front, 76mm side, 51mm rear
M3 Grant	6	384	Turret: 51mm front and sides Hull: 51mm front, 38mm sides and rear
M4A1 Sherman	5	40	Turret: 76mm front (89mm gun mantlet), 51mm sides and rear Hull: 51mm front, 38mm sides and rear

[1] Composite armour 40/30mm basis. The armour thickness is measured at angle from vertical, i.e. the slope of the armour is factored into the thickness, assuming a horizontal strike.

RADIOS

The main radio carried by all British tanks was the Wireless Set No. 11, used for tank-to-tank communications as well as a one-way intercom system that allowed the tank commander to talk to his crew via Tannoy speakers located at each crewman's station. The No. 11 transceiver operated within a frequency range of 4.5 to 7.1 MHz and had a range of between 5km and 32km using 1.8m or 2.7m aerials. The No. 11s would be replaced by the Wireless Set No. 19 (Mk II in 1941, Mk III in 1942), which provided three modes of operation – an 'A' set for long-range communications at the squadron or regimental level, a 'B' set for short-range communications between the tanks of an individual troop, and an 'IC' or internal communication channel that allowed two-way communications between a tank's commander and his crew. The No. 11 set operated on a frequency range of 2–8 MHz ('A' setting) and 229–241 MHz ('B' setting), with a range of 16km for the 'A' set and 900m for the 'B' set between moving vehicles. At this stage of the war there was no dedicated set for communication with accompanying infantry, a practical consequence of doctrinal shortcomings.

US M3 Light, M3 Medium and M4 tanks mostly used the SCR (Signal Corps Radio)-528, an FM transceiver fitted to a platoon commander's tank, whilst the platoon's other four tanks carried SCR-538 receivers – they could not transmit. Both were variants of the 1941-designed SCR-508 and operated on the frequency range of 20–28MHz (making them incompatible with infantry radios); the radios had a maximum range of 24km, though 8km was more realistic on an average day. The predecessor of the SCR-508 sets was the SCR-245, still used in a number of M3/M5 light tanks as well as some medium M3s despite its bulk; operating on a frequency range of 2.0–4.5MHz, it had a maximum range of 72km for continuous wave and 32km for voice transmissions.

British and American tank designations[1]
Tank, Cruiser, Mk I (A9), and Mk I CS
Tank, Cruiser, Mk II (A10), and Mk II CS
Tank, Cruiser, Mk III and Mk IV (A13 Mk I and Mk II)
Tank, Cruiser, Mk VI (A15) Crusader I, and Mk VI CS
Tank, Cruiser, Mk VIA (A15) Crusader II, and Mk VIA CS
Tank, Cruiser, Crusader III (6-pdr)
Tank, Infantry, Mk IIA (A12) Matilda II, and Mk IV CS
Tank, Infantry, Mk III, Valentine II–V (2-pdr), and III CS
Tank, Infantry, Valentine IX (6-pdr)
Tank, Infantry, Mk IV (A22) Churchill (6-pdr)
Light Tank, M2A4 (Stuart I), M3 (Stuart II), M3A1 (Stuart III), M5/M5A1 (Stuart VI)
Medium Tank, M3 (Grant I), M3A5 (Grant II)
Medium Tank, M4 (Sherman I), M4A1 (Sherman II), M4A2 (Sherman III)
[1] Restricted to those versions that featured heavily in the North African and Tunisian campaigns.

GERMAN

The 8.8cm L/56 had rifling that increased from one turn in 45-cal. to one in 30-cal. with a total of 32 grooves. The RA 9's half-length outer tube was fitted with a breech securing collar that prevented movement of the sleeve and inner tube. The inner tube section near the breech had no rifling because it included the unrifled chamber. The three sections of the inner tube were not equal in length; the front section was two-thirds of the length of the rifled section and was more easily replaced than the entire barrel. The horizontal breech mechanism slid to the right to expose the open chamber when loading a shell and slid back to lock the shell prior to firing. The loader could operate the breech actuating mechanism to open and close the breech, or when in the semi-automatic mode the action of loading a shell powered the breech actuating mechanism to close the breech mechanically. When the breech was opened prior to the initial round being loaded, the breech operating lever needed to be grasped and the trigger squeezed to release the retaining catch. The lever was rotated clockwise. If the semi-automatic mode was engaged, a strong pull to rotate the actuating lever was necessary. The semi-automatic catch was engaged by pulling down on the catch plunger and raising the catch to engage the breech actuating mechanism; pressing down disengaged the catch.

When the gun fired, the breech opened, the percussion mechanism was cocked and the counter-recoil of the gun extracted the cartridge case. The breech closed by the cartridge case hitting the extractors, thereby releasing the breech block to close because of the force of the spring actuating mechanism. When firing was completed, the

breech was closed by rotating the extractor actuating lever in a clockwise direction or operating the loading tray interlock without a round in the tray. If the breech block was not fully closed, the detonation of the round in a partially opened breech would lead to the destruction of the gun and crew casualties.

FlaK L/56 and FlaK L/74 shell penetration			
Ammunition type	Weight (projectile)	Velocity	Penetration in mm at 30° angle
Pzgr. Patr.[1]	9.52kg	795m/s	97/100m 93/500m 87/1,000m 80/1,500m 72/2,000m
Pzgr. Patr. 39[2]	10.2kg	800m/s	120/100m 110/500m 100/1,000m 91/1,500m 64/2,000m
Pzgr. Patr. 40[3]	7.27kg	935m/s	170/100m 155/500m 138/1,000m 122/1,500m 110/2,000m
Pzgr. Patr. 39 FlaK 41[4]	9.52kg	980m/s	194/100m 177/500m 159/1,000m 142/1,500m 127/2,000m
Pzgr. Patr. 40 FlaK 41[5]	7.27kg	1,125m/s	237/100m 216/500m 192/1,000m 171/1,500m 152/2,000m

[1] Norris 2002, p. 18.
[2] Gander 2012, p. 67.
[3] Ibid.
[4] Piekalkiewicz 1992, p. 182.
[5] Ibid.

A hydro-pneumatic system operated the recoil. The recuperator cylinder on top of the barrel comprised two cylinders: a liquid cylinder filled with thick glycerine water sitting within the gas cylinder filled with nitrogen. When the gun recoiled, a rod and piston forced liquid from the liquid cylinder into the gas cylinder; the compressed gases partially absorbed the recoil energy with the recoil cylinder absorbing the rest. When the gun completed the recoil, the gas expanded and forced the liquid back into the liquid cylinder, helping the gun to be ready to fire. A scale would show the length

8.8CM FLAK 18 L/56 SIGHTS

For direct fire the 4 x power telescopic sights (Zielfernrohr) ZF.20 or ZF.20E (the former of which lacked a range drum) were used for laying the gun in azimuth and elevation. The ZF.20E – consisting of an elbow telescope, telescope mount and range drum – was mounted on a bracket geared to the elevation quadrant on the right-hand side of the top carriage. The gun was laid in elevation by matching its pointer on the elevation quadrant against a pointer controlled by the telescopic sight. Deflection was set on the gun's deflection drum, with fine tuning estimated through the reticle; 10 mils (18 mils to one degree) from the thin crosshairs to the tip of the inverted 'V' chevron aiming point, 40 mils from the chevron to the thick crosshairs. The ZF.20E provided a 17' 30" field of view in a reticle that could be illuminated by a lamp attachment. The sight also included four lens filters (clear, green, light neutral, dark neutral) to aid in target acquisition during different light conditions. The gun could also use directors for AA use. A Rundblickfernrohr panoramic sight for indirect fire was also mounted on the top of the gun's recuperator tube.

of recoil to make sure the mechanism was working properly. The recoil cylinder below the barrel was filled with 9.5L of fluid; when the gun was recoiling, the cylinder and its control rod stayed stationary, while the piston rod and counter-recoil rod moved within the breech ring. As the gun went back into position, the fluid in the recoil cylinder was forced through apertures in the piston rod head and grooves in the recoil control rod, and by doing so the recoil force was absorbed. When firing horizontally, at 0° of elevation, the recoil was 105cm. The total weight of the gun's parts driven backwards was 1,435kg.

The gun carriage had either pneumatic or sometimes solid rubber tyres. The wheels on the front could be steered and the driver of the prime mover, using the brake pedal, operated the air brakes on all the wheels. To unlimber the gun, jacks on the lower carriage deployed to relieve the pressure of the gun prior to the bogies being disconnected. A winch with lifting chain was mounted above the axles. When the gun was emplaced the outriggers were folded down to create a stable firing platform. Metal stakes were driven into the ground through struts. A screw levelling jack at the end of the outrigger allowed the gun to be set evenly on uneven ground. Hand wheels could also be used to level the top carriage, as the gun trunnions needed to be horizontal prior to the gun firing.

The gun was loaded by placing the shell on the loading tray and then swinging the tray in line with the axis of the bore of the gun. The loading tray interlock was then released and the expanding gas forced the rammer cylinder back along the piston, rapidly withdrawing the rammer. The loader swung the tray back to the loading position. If the loading tray was set on automatic, the round was fired when the tray cleared the path of the recoil. If not on automatic, the firing lever on the left side of the cradle needed to be raised or the auxiliary lever on the right side of the cradle pulled. If a misfire happened, the percussion mechanism was set again, and the rotating lever was rotated in an anticlockwise direction. If a further misfire happened, the crew needed to unload after a short interval by opening the breech. If the extractor failed to eject the shell, the cartridge base had to be physically wrenched out. The fuse setter on the left side of the carriage, to set time-activated fuses, was used by placing a shell into either of two ports.

The ZF.20E telescopic sight was mounted on a bracket in front of the gunner's seat on the right side of the gun. A 17° 30' field of view was given. Sighting was aided by the application of coloured filters – clear, green, light neutral and dark neutral – into the viewfinder by rotating a switch, depending upon climatic and daylight conditions. The sight had to be aligned with the gun prior to the sight being used to direct fire. The gunner used an elevation quadrant featuring a curved metal scale and scale pointer that was graduated in 0.25° intervals. The gunner tracked the target with the traversing wheel. The 0.7m Model 34 rangefinder provided range values via twin lenses that produced two images of a target; when the operator used a range dial, the images would focus into a single image; when this happened, the operator read the range and passed it onto the gun team.

Cartridge cases needed to be strong in order not to rupture on firing and flexible to expand to create a gas-tight seal in the chamber. The case needed to be rust free and watertight in order to keep propellant dry. In the base was either a C/12nA St percussion primer detonated by the firing pin or the C/22 electrically fired primer. The former was used with the FlaK 18/36/37 and 41.

THE COMBATANTS

BRITISH

The interwar army determined to utilize technology rather than manpower to avoid the losses of World War I; the army would be small, highly mobile and professional, and would have the best weapons available. In the training manuals the use of multiple waves was advised, despite some advocating that infiltration should be used to create opportunities neighbouring units could exploit. Scientific solutions were sought to the application of military force, and because the belief was that the progress of battles could be predicted, thorough planning would mitigate all different courses of enemy action. Senior officers would ensure the coordination of different arms; however, this would be to the detriment of allowing junior officers to take advantage of fleeting opportunities.

In the German army the opposite was true. To ensure that multiple approaches were not adopted, field training taught officers to implement drills. The Germans taught common solutions. In Britain this went against freedom of choice; senior

A gun crew prepares their 5cm PaK 38 (L/60) AT gun for action in the Western Desert, c.1941. The PaK 38 was an effective tank killer – its standard 2.25kg Pzgr. round could punch through 60mm of armour at 1,000m – and made up the backbone of the DAK's AT screen for the first years of the campaign. Le Quesne Martel looked into Operation *Crusader* and thought combined arms were needed to destroy German armoured formations; however, studies stressed defensive measures and did not point out the aggressive use of enemy AT guns. The British failed to work out the proper loss rate of German tanks, and also underestimated the Italians, assuming that they could not fight effectively. (SeM/Universal Images Group via Getty Images)

35

A Stuart tank is silhouetted against the setting sun as its commander scans the horizon, 6 September 1942. In January 1942 the three regiments of 2nd Armoured Brigade were each given a company of riflemen, a battery of field guns and troop of AT guns from the Divisional Support Group, and then relieved 7th Armoured Division near Agedabia. When Rommel attacked, the brigade was short of petrol and, split into regimental groups to fight three separate battles, suffered accordingly. Supply echelon lorries from the 9th Lancers narrowly escaped capture, and were able to refuel tanks. By the end of the month the 9th Lancers had ten Crusaders and ten M3s, whilst the 10th Hussars made do with a composite squadron of seven tanks. On 3 February the 9th Lancers, with replacement vehicles, was nearly back to full strength with 47 tanks. (Sgt. A.W. Ackland/Imperial War Museums via Getty Images)

officers were permitted to interpret how doctrine was to be implemented and because each regiment trained its officers, different approaches would be taught. The British wanted to develop better communications in order not to rely on junior officer initiative. Definite tasks were allotted to units and certain discretion was given in how to achieve the task; however, if the task was no longer relevant then this needed to be reported prior to permission being given to follow a new approach. Also the need to defend a newly captured position against counterattack prevented the rapid exploitation of opportunities won. This approach was thought to help maintain morale. Setting defined objectives would prevent physical and moral exhaustion. Orders were detailed and written above divisional level; however, mobile encounter battles would be prolific and would need orders to be sent rapidly.

In December 1941 the British report on the 'Second Libyan Campaign', Operation *Crusader*, admitted that armoured units were ignorant about the use of heavy FlaK guns in the AT role in the numbers they encountered; the report thought that armoured tactics did not include provision to defeat this new threat. As early as March 1942 Eighth Army HQ reported on the role of armoured formations in battle and noted that the highest losses to German armour were incurred when they drove towards British guns. This also happened when British tanks following German armour encountered German AT guns. The report stated that this should be avoided; however, the 2-pdr gun on the cruisers could not penetrate the strengthened armour on the front of the Panzer III and IV. British armoured formations had to charge to close the range. This played into German AT gun tactics that encouraged such a move.

The lessons of Operation *Crusader* were not on the whole passed on because 182,200 new soldiers arrived in the Middle East between January and August 1942, and the usual method was to replace whole battalions and sometimes whole divisions in the front line. Auchinleck, realizing the problem, had asked that drafts rather than new formations be sent. The dissemination of intelligence about the enemy was poor and there was not enough time to brief the new arrivals properly. The armoured crews

ATTACK ON A GERMAN POSITION

The attacking British Armoured Regiment's squadrons are organized in a 'one up' formation, the traditional deployment when attempting to drive through an enemy line. Each squadron has three troops (**A**, **B** and **C**), comprising Crusader IIs and Crusader Close Support versions with 3in. howitzer (blue) and M3 Grants (green), advancing in the same 'one up' formation, their tanks 100m apart (though in reality this distance varied greatly). The Regimental HQ (**D**) is at the centre of the formation. The importance of infantry support was by now understood, and it was common to have a motorized company (**E**) attached to individual regiments. In addition, each regiment could rely on direct support from an artillery battery of eight 25-pdr guns (**F**). As well as firing HE shells to suppress enemy infantry and gun crews, the 25-pdrs were expected to lay down copious amounts of smoke, as would the pair of 3in. howitzer-equipped CS tanks attached to the armoured regiment's headquarters.

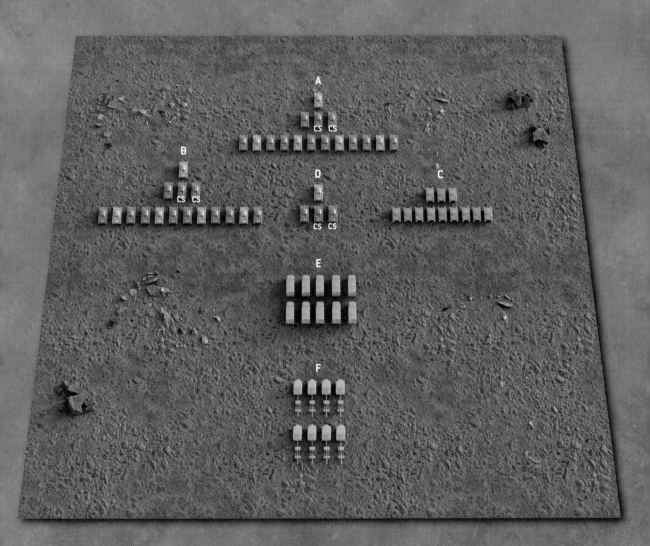

An M3 'Honey' light tank, outdistancing its own supply vehicles, draws petrol from an RAF bowser, *c.*1942. The 2nd Royal Gloucestershire Hussars landed in Egypt on 1 October 1941. Noticing the M3 Stuarts on the dock, they were initially grateful they were not issued with them; however, they would find the M3 engines to be better than those in their cruisers. Three weeks of exercise were followed by deployment to the front. On 16 November, news arrived that Operation *Crusader* would commence soon. Additional training for formations when they reached theatre was curtailed. Training in the UK made them confident, and they thought there was not much else to learn. (The Print Collector/Getty Images)

A low-profile FlaK 18 firing at British tanks, October 1941. On a still day, a furrow could be seen made by the 8.8cm shell speeding a few feet above the ground, indicating where the guns were located. The Pzgr. 39 shell made a neat hole in the armour and then detonated, filling the turret with chunks of flying metal. If the hull was hit, the shell could wound or kill the crew, ignite the tank's ammunition or enter the engine compartment and set the petrol ablaze. Until the appearance of the American M3 and M4 medium tanks with their 75mm guns, there was little chance of the 2-pdr-armed cruisers or infantry tanks being able to worry heavy FlaK positions, especially when they were dug in — concealment was the best option. British tactics in May 1942 stressed the use of smoke by one squadron to shroud the enemy guns, permitting the remaining two squadrons a fighting chance to close with the enemy. (Ullstein Bild via Getty Images)

in particular were not properly informed and thought heavy FlaK was responsible for more losses than the gun caused. A report in March 1942 by the Deputy Prime Minister Clement Attlee looked at 48 tanks rendered unserviceable during Operation *Crusader*. Only 14 were damaged by heavy FlaK, with seven damaged by 5cm guns, three by the 3.7cm gun and 24 by lighter weapons, mines or mechanical breakdown. In July 1942 the Germans, aware of this fear, used telegraph poles to create dummy heavy FlaK guns. The dominance of German AT gun tactics was evidenced at El Alamein in October 1942 when the Germans still had 400 weapons of 5cm calibre and higher. Middle East Training Manual No. 7 stated that the battle was borne by the infantry tackling the gun line.

Crusaders in the Western Desert, c.1941–42. In September 1941, 2nd Armoured Brigade, comprising 2nd Bays, 10th Hussars and 9th Lancers, followed 22nd Armoured Brigade out to the desert. The brigade had the same regiments since formation in 1937. The 9th Lancers were told they would be given M3 light tanks; only troop leaders had the new Mark VI cruisers, and liked their powered traverse and Liberty engines. M3s were thought of as old-fashioned and uncomfortable, with an engine that spluttered; however, the M3 hardly ever broke, and its 37mm was no worse than the 2-pdr on the cruiser. On 28 September, with seven Crusaders and 17 M3s, the 9th Lancers departed; they would receive 28 tanks when they arrived in Suez on 28 November, but not in time for Operation Crusader. (AFP via Getty Images)

Even in 1942 many senior commanders persisted with exerting authority on their juniors and stayed back from the front. Some during Operation *Crusader* had a tactical HQ forward. Lieutenant-General William Gott was in a tank forward of his Advanced HQ. GHQ discouraged this behaviour. Lieutenant-General Frank Messervy was captured in May 1942 when his Advanced HQ was destroyed, though he soon escaped. Commanders did not always radiate authority. General Neil Ritchie held long meetings during operations where he listened to advice from his subordinates and then did not give precise orders. In eliminating Rommel's force, effectively surrounded in the Gazala Cauldron, 5th Indian and 7th Armoured divisions commanded by different formations did not cooperate because neither wanted to be responsible. Ritchie failed to assign responsibility. During the Gazala fighting the commanders of 1st and 7th Armoured divisions, Major-General Herbert Lumsden and Messervy, did not get on. Many did not have experience in armoured warfare in the desert. Auchinleck was an Indian Army officer and needed his Military Secretary to advise him on appointments. Ritchie, a divisional commander, was promoted beyond his capabilities. The movements of the British brigades were disjointed and lacked coordination by division with, in some instances, junior commanders ignoring orders or protesting.

The 8th King's Royal Irish Hussars of 4th Armoured Brigade training with their new American M3 Stuart 'Honey' light tanks on 28 August 1941 near Gebel el Kashab in the Western Desert. The 2nd Armoured Brigade spent two weeks in Egypt firing-in their guns at local ranges. On the approach march to the front, the M3s were fine; however, the cruisers, covering 160km per day, frequently broke down when water pumps leaked. Petrol was scarce, and the brigade had to stop on 22 December for a week. (Hulton Archive/Getty Images)

A Matilda II advances in support of accompanying infantry, c.1941. British infantry relied on artillery and tanks to provide firepower needed to manoeuvre across the battlefield because their support weapons could not generate the sustained firepower of their German equivalents. However, field guns were organized at divisional level into two heavy batteries and could not rapidly be called in, and infantry tanks with their machine guns could destroy enemy MG positions, not enemy AT positions, as the 2-pdr could not fire HE. (Felix Man/Picture Post/ Hulton Archive/Getty Images)

Montgomery (who arrived to command Eighth Army in September 1942), by stressing the main objective, imposed authority on the battlefield. Training enabled familiarity with the rigours of the battlefield. Battle inoculation, applied gradually, familiarized men with the battlefield's sights and sound. Solutions to common battlefield problems were taught as battle drills.

Personnel were chosen more carefully. A War Office study in January 1941 concluded that 50 per cent of Royal Armoured Corps (RAC) personnel did not have the intelligence for full efficiency. In June 1941 a Directorate of Selection of Personnel was established. By November two-thirds of new personnel were being tested, and by July 1942 all personnel. To prove the system was working, 2,000 RAC personnel sent to the Middle East as drafts in the summer of 1942 were looked at; the report found near-perfect allocations of personnel, based on the intelligence needed for the job they had to do, were being sent. Reforms to officer selection improved. In 1941 officer candidates had a short interview, and 20–50 per cent were failing the officer's course. In 1942 cadets had to pass a three-day assessment centre where one in three were rejected. Officers were taught the welfare of their men was their first concern. Such improvements did not offer results until late 1942.

In June 1942 the US produced an intelligence report on the effectiveness of the German 8.8cm heavy FlaK gun on armour during the Battle of Gazala. They concluded that the British were incapable of opposing them and would endeavour to avoid them. The report described the 4th Armoured Brigade attack on Rommel on 27 May as losing 16 Grants, all to 8.8cm gunfire. British tanks were vulnerable at long range and needed to use reverse slopes to cover movement or use extensive artillery preparations of HE and smoke.

GERMAN

The FlaK 18 and 36 were not ideal AT guns because they were high, bulky, heavy and hard to hide. Emplacing the gun took a lot of effort; firing from an open position was dangerous. Loading the gun with the barrel horizontal was not easy for the gunner; the gun was designed for the loader to load with the barrel elevated. Raising a round weighing nearly 15kg to near head height took some effort. Aimers were similarly hampered as they could not easily access their position. Having the gun used on armour in 1940 in France was only supposed to be an improvisation. The inherently flexible-minded German soldiers accepted the use against tanks in France; because doctrine did not exist, they developed procedures in tactical deployment that took notice of the inherent difficulties of using the weapon in this way. In the desert, where the gun could engage at long range from where British crews could not effectively counter them, the best results were achieved.

The crew extensively drilled to ensure they instinctively knew how to operate the gun. Unlimbering from a towed state was practised to have the gun ready to fire within two minutes. When firing on ground targets, K1 was on the elevation mechanism, K2 operated the traverse mechanism and used the optical searching sight to look for targets, and K6 was on the fuse setter if operable.[1] The gun commander and K2 might receive target data from an observer or command post in the form of elevation degree, scale ring number and target distance. K2 would hold the target image in the telescopic sight on the horizontal line of the sight reticule and the gun team would fire. The commander needed to site the gun where the prevailing winds would blow the smoke from the muzzle away from the position in order not to obstruct the target or his ability to issue words of command. When armour was spotted, the commander would give the following command: shell type, target description, elevation angle, sight

---

1   K stands for *Kanonier*, or gunner.

An 8.8cm gun and its crew in a well dug-in position before Sollum, 17 June 1941. (Ullstein Bild via Getty Images)

8.8CM FLAK L/56 CREW

A well-trained and full-strength crew could have their gun set up and ready for action in under 2½ minutes with a maximum rate of fire of 15rpm. The ten-strong crew of a FlaK 18/36/37 were commanded by a Geschützführer and nine Kanoniere numbered K1 to K9; each gun also had a driver for the prime mover, usually an SdKfz 7 half-track, and a pair of guns were under the command of a Zugführer. The crew's roles when the gun was engaging ground targets were as follows:

Geschützführer (GF). He would often be near the K2 so that he could take over target acquisition if the gunner failed to identify the enemy quickly enough.

K1. Layer for elevation.
K2. Layer for line (traverse) and Z.F.20E optical sight.
K3. Loader.
K4. Ammunition handler/spotter.
K5. Ammunition handler/spotter.
K6. Fuse-setting machine operator.
K7. Fuse setter (machine loader).
K8. Ammunition handler/spotter.
K9. Ammunition handler/spotter.

angle. The commander could sight the gun for K2 if K2 did not find the target following this description. The barrel, breech and even traverse and elevation handles would be painful to touch. During the warmest daylight hours heat haze could obscure the target and judging range was difficult because of the lack of prominent features. Rangefinders were essential, as the haze would encourage gunners to think vehicles were closer than they thought, yet even with these, when close to the ground, a flat view could lead to optical distortion.

In early 1941 I./FlaK 33 deployed with Rommel to Libya, closely followed by I./FlaK 18 in July. In September 1941 the FlaK-Regiment to command the two FlaK units was established when the staff and support personnel arrived. The commander, Major Hecht, had fought in the desert since the beginning of the campaign. Oberleutnant Rudolf Marwan-Schlosser in October commanded I./FlaK 18. On 2 November Hecht and Marwan-Schlosser reported to Oberstleutnant Heymer, the Luftwaffe commander. Heymer told them he was not interested in using their guns on air targets. The regiment instead was to report to Crüwell, the Panzergruppe commander, not the Luftwaffe commander. Major Fischer's II./FlaK 25, shipped to North Africa in June 1941, was already weakened with 7./FlaK 25 sunk on the merchant

ship *Caffero* by a torpedo from a British plane. The personnel were rescued and 7./FlaK 25 would reach North Africa with its guns only in May 1942; in November 1941, 6. and 8.Batterie were brought to Tobruk and incorporated into the FlaK-Regiment. In the spring I./FlaK 43 and I./FlaK 6 would be brought in to increase gun strength and batteries would have six rather than four guns. On 6 July Oberst Alwin Wolz (the new commander) told Rommel that the regiment had grown beyond the capacity of the maintenance crews to look after the guns. The regiment grew to a division. There were 128 officers, 650 NCOs and 3,666 men, 32 heavy and 72 light FlaK guns, and nine quad 2cm guns on half-tracks. In July, I./FlaK 53 also joined them. In August 1942, I./FlaK 46 then arrived.

Luftwaffe heavy FlaK units primarily would support the DAK; however, there were also Heeres-FlaKartillerie-Abteilungen. The 10.Panzer-Division, when transferred to Tunisia in late 1942, had three batteries of heavy FlaK in its artillery unit, which in April 1943 was established as Heeres-FlaKartillerie-Abteilung 302 with four 8.8cm guns and three 2cm guns per battery. Also in Tunisia was I./FlaK 54 with von Arnim, and II./FlaK 52 deployed there in November 1942. In Tunis and Bizerta 20.FlaK-Division had, in the defence of the port and city,

A FlaK 18 in Cyrenaica, October 1941. The Geschützführer (standing to the right of the gun) and his Kanoniere stand ready for action. The physical effort needed to operate the gun in a hot desert environment from an emplaced position with camouflage netting, plus the heat from the gun, took its toll on the crew. Dysentery was rife and crews would be reduced below establishment. (Ullstein Bild via Getty Images)

An '88' firing on British forces, 1941. The movement of massed columns of vehicles coupled with the explosions of both enemy and friendly guns served to throw dust and smoke into the air, obscuring attempts at targeting. Ranging shots that did not hit would create a screen for the enemy to hide behind. In addition, firing the gun could identify its position, because when the '88' was employed against ground targets, the low muzzle depression created a highly visible dust trail. Crews found firing from the wheels safer in order to change position if observed. (Ullstein Bild via Getty Images)

A heavy FlaK crew in action – note the black warhead of the shell, denoting it as a Pzgr. 39 AP round. There was little time for training. New crews were used as munitions carriers to experience combat, and would occupy other crew positions when casualties occurred. Training on the job in this way was not ideal. Infantry skills were of increasing importance, and each gun had an MG for close protection. Younger recruits were found to be prone to illness in the harsh climate; replacements were not tested to see if they could withstand the environment before being sent, with the result that many had to be sent home. Drivers in particular were in short supply and had to be borrowed from the Heer. (Ullstein Bild via Getty Images)

FlaK-Regiment 78 with static FlaK-Abteilungen 372 and 503. These guns would be used against ground units in May 1943. In November FlaK-Regiment Hermann Göring arrived in Tunisia with six heavy batteries, each of four 8.8cm guns and three 2cm guns.

Muzzle covers on the guns were a necessity to prevent barrel rifling from being disrupted by sand. The breech block was kept wrapped in fabric when the gun was not in use to exclude particles interfering with its closing or stopping the firing pin making a good contact with the primer in the base of the shell. Daily crew tasks included the inspection of the bore for any signs of rust, significant wear or damage, and presence of dirt, debris and fouling. Every time the gun was in action, the barrel had to be cleaned with a mixture of water and sodium bicarbonate, dried out with sponges and lightly oiled; however, sparse oil and grease were applied because too much could attract dust. Bore liner sections might have to be replaced once the inner bore tube was pushed out to clean.

The breech block was also cleaned and the gunner would operate the mechanism to test smooth operation. If the mechanism did not function properly, the crew would disassemble and clean the parts, then put them back together. The gunner also ensured that the firing pin could hit the base of the cartridge case effectively. Traverse and elevation wheels needed sufficient lubrication to work properly. Recuperator cylinders had to have sufficient gas pressure and liquid levels to operate the mechanism. Recharging and refilling needed the system drained of both gas and liquid. Liquid levels needed to be checked in the recoil cylinder, too. If the gun was slamming back abruptly rather than smoothly, this would be a sign something was wrong. The gas pressure and liquid levels in the rammer assembly were checked, as was the rammer tray for wear and tear. Hinges on the mount, especially the outriggers, needed proper lubrication. On the limber, the tyre pressure and power brake air line connections needed regular examination.

FLAK 88 DEFENCE

A battery of four (later six) 8.8cm guns when deploying in the AT role would not use the same 'square' pattern required in AA defence. The guns would deploy in a spaced line, the exact positions of individual guns determined by terrain and projected fields of fire. Often guns would be deployed as part of a FlaKkampftruppe, a flexible battlefield formation based around a four- or six-gun battery and supporting elements, though smaller deployments of a single Zug were common. To ensure a degree of mutual support, and in situations that required a tactical advance or retreat bounding overwatch would be employed, the first Zug providing cover whilst the second Zug broke down its guns, moved, set up in a new position, and provided cover in turn for the first Zug during its move.

This diagram (not to scale) shows the two guns of an emplaced 8.8cm Zug; each 8.8cm gun (**1**) forms the anchor of a strongpoint and is set up in the centre of a triangular configuration, and sighted for 360° fields of fire (Millen 2014, p. 9). Each 8.8cm gun site is defended by two outlying forward positions (**2**) equipped with either one of the Abteilung's 2cm FlaK 38 guns, an anti-tank gun (usually a 5cm PaK 38) or an MG34 on a tripod mount. A further position behind the gun (**3**) would contain a mortar (8cm Granatwerfer 34). Communication trenches (**4**) would be dug connecting all the positions together, allowing the commander (C, located near the 8.8cm gun) to redeploy his weapons as the situation warranted.

A Mittlerer Zugkraftwagen 8t (SdKfz 7) towing a FlaK 18, Raum Bardia or Sidi Omar, 19 September 1941. The gun's SdKfz 7 prime mover had a 50–70 per cent-reduced engine lifespan in the desert, as sand intruded into working parts and vehicles were driven in low gears. They created a dust haze that made them easy to spot from aircraft. (Bundesarchiv, BA 101I-433-0892-23)

In September 1942 Marwan-Schlosser wrote a report that assessed the heavy FlaK. He thought the guns should not be used in the ground AT role all the time. If this happened, the crews would lose their proficiency when called to fire on air targets. Marian-Schlosser in another report wrote that guns in the front line were highly vulnerable; they needed a lot of maintenance because breakages were common. Using the gun on aircraft needed specialist devices that were hard to obtain and highly sensitive. He urged guns should be designated for use against either tanks or aircraft. A battery used on aircraft should be used against tanks only in an emergency; in theory they needed permission to revert to a ground role; however, in practice battery commanders targeted tanks immediately when they appeared.

Marwan-Schlosser wrote that guns should be sited 100m apart. Target priorities on the ground were: the most dangerous, the closest, and then whatever was closest to their aiming point. Multiple guns firing on the most dangerous target was acceptable. The battery needed to change position only if enemy guns brought down heavy fire on their position. Shooting from the trailer was preferable, as rapid changes of position could be needed; however, a reduction in precision and higher miss rate meant higher expenditure of rounds and the trailer might suffer damage. Only if the gun was static would the struts be laid out. Trailer fire was essential when the Grant with its 75mm gun appeared. To survive, the heavy FlaK needed the support of all weapons. Shooting later was preferable in order to secure a higher probability of hitting. The British, he noticed, were attempting to get the crews to engage early; in order to evade the fire of heavy FlaK, they attacked with smoke shells.

When marching, vehicles needed to be 100m from each other. If enemy tanks were in the vicinity, they would follow friendly tanks in a staggered formation. Ammunition lorries marched behind the guns. The guns were accompanied by 2cm light batteries to guard against enemy planes. Heavy guns should not be used in the spearhead because they were slow. Movement at night was better done in moonlight; much less fuel was expended at low speeds during poor visibility. Night lights should be used only to find missing vehicles.

SERGEANT BILL CLOSE

Bill Close joined the RTC in 1933 and in 1934 was sent to 3rd Royal Tank Regiment. In May 1940 he was a sergeant in France and fought at Calais, where he escaped capture. He sailed to Egypt late that year, where his unit joined 2nd Armoured Division. In early 1941, 3rd Royal Tank Regiment went to Greece with 4th Hussars, where they lost most of their A-10 tanks; Close was evacuated to Crete then Egypt, where the unit was equipped with the M3 Stuart. He was a squadron sergeant-major when 3rd Royal Tank Regiment of 4th Armoured Brigade fought in Operation *Crusader* in November 1941; officer casualties were high and Close was commissioned because he had been awarded a DCM. He was given No. 3 troop in A Squadron (the Recce Squadron).

On 27 May 1942 his tank was hit in the front, and with only the driver slightly wounded the crew changed tanks. His force would increase in strength to 15 Grants and 14 Stuarts as stragglers were found, but the unit was ambushed at the top of an escarpment and Close's tank was again hit – within a few minutes only six Grants and five Stuarts were left. The 3rd Royal Tank Regiment was soon withdrawn to Egypt where Close was promoted captain and made second in command of his squadron. That summer he was wounded when a 75mm shell hit his tank, setting it on fire; though he was in hospital for four weeks, he recovered in time for El Alamein. The 3rd Royal Tank Regiment was now part of 10th Armoured Division. He helped with the training of the other units of the new 8th Armoured Brigade that were ex-cavalry (3rd Royal Tank Regiment had one squadron of 2-pdr Crusaders and two with Shermans). On 26 March 1943 they had infantry from the 2nd New Zealand Division ride on their tanks through German positions on the Mareth Line, eventually leaving Tunisia in December. Close would fight in Normandy in the summer of 1944 and stayed with his unit until the end of the war, commanding his squadron.

The use of guns in a set-piece attack must not be done from the front line. The guns should be kept mobile in order to move them if smoke targeted them. Mobile guns could move rapidly to where the main enemy tank attack was launched. The infantry needed to protect the guns, but Italian infantry could not be relied upon to do this. He now advised that guns should be positioned to fire 200–300m apart, with 2cm guns between them. Where entrenched, guns should be entrenched to the barrel. The floor of the entrenchment was to be covered by sandbags in the direction of fire in order to reduce the formation of dust. Stones needed to be set in concrete in order to be useful. Crews needed personal weapons and would occupy shelters 50m from the guns. Guns needed to have 360° of coverage. Bases needed to have enough rounds to sustain prolonged defence. A radio connection between bases was to be established. Decoy guns would make ideal targets for artillery. Decoys could also be used to deceive planes. Fire should be rapid to make enemy forces think that more guns occupied the position. Better radios were needed to transmit uninterrupted over long distance. Marwan-Schlosser recommended using a recon vehicle as a mobile observation platform. Aiming guns in the desert was difficult; 6x30 binoculars were insufficient; 70x50 or 10x50 were needed. All-round base defence to the last round was expected, as the arrival of a relief force was likely in the desert.

In April 1943 a training specifications manual made various points about the tactical movement and use of the gun against ground targets. Crews were told to fire from the chassis principally and expend additional shells to compensate for a loss in accuracy. Frequent changes of position needed to be made of at least 100m in order to force the enemy to change aim. The integration of the guns with

GEFREITER ARNOLD HÜBNER

Born on 14 July 1919 at Szubin, Posen, Arnold Hübner was the son of a schoolteacher. After completing his education, Arnold began his compulsory service with the Reichsarbeitsdienst in April 1939, and five months later he was drafted into the Luftwaffe, joining Luftwaffe-Bau Kompanie 13/1. He served in the Polish campaign and on 12 April 1940 transferred to the FlaKartillerie, where he was promoted to Gefreiter in September and posted to 3.Batterie, I./FlaK-Regiment 33. He moved with his unit to North Africa, where not long after his arrival he took part in successful artillery attacks on British positions at Mersa Brega. Artillerymen were often rewarded for their collective efforts, and for his part in his unit's successes around Agedabia, Hübner was awarded the Iron Cross Second Class on 25 May 1941.

Soon afterwards, his unit played an important role in the defence of Sollum on 16 June. Hübner and his comrades were occupying the pivotal Point 208, a remote rocky hillock far out in the desert which was held by Oberleutnant Ziemer's battery from FlaK-Regiment 33. They endured heavy artillery fire, and shortly after the barrage ended, more than 20 Matilda II infantry tanks from 4th Armoured Brigade attacked; at ranges of only 1,000m a furious exchange of fire continued for at least half an hour, at the end of which eight tanks had been knocked out and the remainder had withdrawn. This was only one of several actions in the general area of Halfaya ('Hellfire') Pass during which the battalion knocked out more than 90 tanks. Hübner was among those recommended for the Iron Cross First Class, awarded on 5 July. By late December 1941 his FlaK battalion was in defensive action around Bardia, where once again Hübner distinguished himself by coolness under fire, his accurate shooting adding a further eight kills to bring his personal score of tanks knocked out to a total of 24. This

performance won him the Knight's Cross, the first private soldier in the Afrika Korps to receive the award. He was promoted to Obergefreiter on 1 June but spent the remainder of the year recovering from illness. He served in a number of training units, eventually being commissioned as Leutnant on 1 May 1945, just a week before the end of the war (Williamson 2005, pp. 20–21).

Gefreiter Arnold Hübner (left) and Unteroffizier Erich Heintze (right) after receiving the Knight's Cross, April 1942. Note Hübner's Anti-Aircraft Flak Battle Badge (Flak-Kampfabzeichen der Luftwaffe) above his belt. (National Digital Archive, Poland)

armour was stressed to bring them into action at the best time. The heavy FlaK guns were seen as particularly effective in covering a retreat on account of their range and firepower. In the offensive, guns sited at 200–300m intervals were sufficiently apart to leave corridors friendly tanks could use to advance through. Guns kept on their wheels could advance forward once they had fired, whilst others also on wheels covered them.

COMBAT

In February 1941 I./FlaK 33 deployed to Tripoli with the rest of 5.Leichte-Division, with I./FlaK 18 joining them in July. In June, south of Halfaya Pass, an infantry company with a 3.7cm AT gun platoon was entrenched on height 208. The 3./FlaK 33 with Oberleutnant Ziemer was with them, behind sandbags with only their barrels above the ground. Ziemer was optimistic about success; his guns had good fields of fire to the east, south-east and south. On 15 June his guards heard tank

A Panzer III in the desert near Tobruk driving back to rear lines, June 1941. Sitting on the hull are three captured British soldiers and a German tank crew member (either from the tank shown or – more likely – from another knocked-out panzer). (Ullstein Bild via Getty Images)

An SdKfz 7 towing heavy FlaK in the Western Desert, sometime in 1941. From late November to 15 December, 3./FlaK-Regiment 33 had covered 1,500km and destroyed 54 enemy tanks, two armoured cars, three gun batteries, six SP guns, four AT guns, eight MG nests and 120 trucks, firing 1,820 rounds. Its casualties totalled one officer and eight men killed, 41 wounded, two men missing and 20 men captured in Bardia. (Bundesarchiv, BA 101I-783-0109-19)

OPPOSITE BOTTOM

Members of the DAK examine the knocked-out shell of a Matilda II to the west of Sollum, June 1941. On the morning of 25 November, when 15.Panzer-Division advanced north-north-west to Sidi Azeiz, a British tank battalion tried to stop it – 16 Matildas and a cruiser were destroyed by 3./FlaK-Regiment 33. An SdKfz 7 was hit and destroyed by enemy gunfire. Losses were two killed and two more wounded. (Ullstein Bild via Getty Images)

noises; the offensive by Wavell to relieve Tobruk had started. The crews were ready to fire in a few minutes. In total 30 tanks were seen in a close group and the battery opened fire. Tanks dispersed in the dust. The British brought down artillery fire on the German defences. Then 70 tanks of 7th Armoured Brigade were seen, and Ziemer, his guns unaffected by the bombardment, let them approach to within 1km. His guns fired, and the British crews fired back; however, when panzers approached, the British armour fled. In the afternoon 40 British tanks in the first wave headed south of height 208, followed by about half that number obscured by a dust cloud in the second wave. Ziemer waited again until they were within a kilometre and then opened fire, hitting many and persuading the rest to retreat. Two tanks had approached closer; one was knocked out within 200m of the battery position with the other driving on a gun trailer and then moving off. On the flank ten tanks were then seen approaching at 5,000m distance; they were scared off by gunfire when two were stopped at 4,000m. In the late afternoon 80 tanks were repelled with the help of German tanks from Panzer-Regiment 5 appearing on the British flank. The British fully realized the heavy FlaK was the cause of the operation's failure. The 6th Royal Tank Regiment lost 30 Crusaders on 15 June.

On 16 June 50 tanks tried to move on Bardia. Oberleutnant Tocki, leading Panzerjäger-Abteilung 33 with one heavy FlaK gun, moved from Bardia; the crew fired at British tanks at 2,000m. Three tanks soon stopped and, having realized heavy FlaK were present, the rest used smoke to cover their retreat when elements of Panzer-Regiment 8 arrived. On 17 June, in Halfaya Pass, heavy FlaK hit 14 tanks. The offensive was stalled. Of the 202 tanks 7th Armoured Division started with, 98 were lost in the operation; in most instances the heavy FlaK prior to German armour intervening had blunted their initial advances.

In September 1941, 1. and 2.Batterie of both FlaK 18 (Hauptmann Drossow) and FlaK 33 (Hauptmann Fromm) were deployed in the ground role in Halfaya Pass. The

3.Batterie of FlaK 18 and FlaK 33 were used on aircraft in the defence of Bardia. The 4. and 5.Batterie of FlaK 18 with 2cm guns defended 15.Panzer-Division from attack by low-flying aircraft. The 4. and 5.Batterie of FlaK 33 guarded airfields and harbours. On 10 November, new heavy guns arrived and replaced old guns; eight of the latter were formed into 1a. and 2a.Batterie FlaK 18, with two guns each in four positions supporting Italian positions on the front line. With news of a British offensive in the offing, in mid-November 3./FlaK 33 was sent to 15.Panzer-Division, 3./FlaK 18 was sent to 21.Panzer-Division, 2./FlaK 18 was sent to join Aufklärungs-Abteilung 33 near Tobruk, and 1./FlaK 18 with Marwan-Schlosser was stationed at the boundary of 15. and 21.Panzer-Division.

The British were about to launch Operation *Crusader*. Gott's 7th Armoured Division had 7th, 22nd and 4th Armoured brigades. British doctrine thought infantry always needed armoured protection and this led to the fragmentation of 7th Armoured Division. There was 32km between 4th and 7th Armoured brigades because the former was asked to guard the flank of the infantry advancing by the sea. 1st South African Division farther inland needed armour to guard against Italian tanks and in this role 22nd Armoured Brigade would be miles from Gabr Saleh, where the British planned to engage German armour. Gabr Saleh was not an important enough location to lure Rommel. Sidi Rezegh was preferred; however, this was farther from the infantry that 4th Armoured Brigade was asked to support. Rommel did not even realize that enemy armour was moving on Gabr Saleh because the rains had grounded his aerial reconnaissance. The British plan was faulty; how

Wavell, Commander-in-Chief India, meeting with Auchinleck, Commander-in-Chief Middle East, to discuss the war situation, January 1941. Eighth Army never had the same commanders for long – there were six in 16 months. There was also a proliferation of formations or parts of formations. Whilst 7th Armoured Division had trained together prior to the war, new formations had not developed common methods. A loss of command functionality was often the result of personnel or units within a brigade being transferred after they had established a way of working together. Experience was lost, lessons were not learnt and tactical policy did not develop. The Germans rapidly destroyed inexperienced formations, like 1st Armoured Division. There needed to be standard drills to meet typical situations, and these took time to develop. (James Jarche/The LIFE Picture Collection via Getty Images)

Heavy FlaK on the move near El Alamein, July 1942. On 27 November 1941, the 2cm guns with 3./FlaK-Regiment 33 suppressed enemy machine guns and enabled the battery's three 8.8cm guns to move into position. In the afternoon, whilst moving to Gambut, 15.Panzer-Division encountered strong enemy forces 16km to the south-west of the town. The battery was sent to the hard-pressed area. Nine tanks were destroyed. (Bundesarchiv, BA 101I-444-1672-04)

they would respond to Rommel's movements would show their inability to respond to a fluid and changing situation.

Rommel advanced with his panzer divisions on the now isolated 7th Armoured Brigade at Sidi Rezegh. On 21 November 1941 Panzer-Regiment 8, its ammunition expended, first had to break off contact. The FlaK guns of 3./FlaK 33 stopped the advance of pursuing British tanks, in two days destroying ten by firing 100 rounds. By the beginning of 22 November British tank number superiority was wiped out. The British lost 180 tanks, most of them at Sidi Rezegh, and the Germans and Italians 20. Both sides now had 300 tanks. On the morning of 23 November, 20km south-east of El Adem, two 8.8cm guns of the same battery firing 107 rounds destroyed four tanks and 20 trucks. The battery was on the wing next to the Italian Armoured Division Ariete; however, because of the rapid advance of the German armour ordered by Rommel to envelop south and then north to Sidi Rezegh, the Italians could not maintain contact with them. The British noticed this and launched armour with guns and infantry against them, where the 8.8cm guns were positioned. The guns destroyed five cruisers, two armoured cars, 20 trucks and field guns with 135 shells, both AP and HE; a half-track with Type 201 trailer was destroyed by British artillery fire, and two men were killed and two wounded.

Meanwhile, by 1430hrs the panzer divisions linked with the Ariete and began to move north. They were between 1st and 5th South African brigades. Gott, with 5th South African Brigade the previous night, ordered guns to the south to defend this approach; in the box 46 25-pdrs were dispersed to fire on tanks. At 1600hrs the Axis attacked on a 16km stretch. There was a swamp to the south of them and the Germans were being fired at from the south and north. The shallow depth of the position precluded a proper attack formation. The Germans tried to stay in their vehicles and were met with a withering fire; 72 tanks were lost. The battle showed that infantry brigades could inflict severe losses on enemy tanks. Guns could be effective in destroying enemy armour; however, the South Africans persisted in thinking that giving tanks to infantry formations was needed. On 26 November Auchinleck installed Major-General Sir Neil Ritchie as the new Eighth Army commander; Ritchie was Deputy Chief of Staff. The British by then had suffered 800 tank losses and the crews began to lose confidence in their ability to defeat their opponent without being demoralized by unsustainable casualties.

An Eighth Army officer examines the remains of a FlaK 18 put out of action by British artillery near Bir el Gobi, 30km south-west of Gambut in Cyrenaica, 28 November 1941. That day's battery records show the FlaK B gun of 3./FlaK-Regiment 33 was damaged and a connecting pin on the FlaK D gun trailer hitch broke during a long-range exchange with enemy tanks and guns. The next day, with an SdKfz 7 hit and unable to be repaired, only a single gun could fire. On 30 November three guns were again operable, and, with no enemy tanks to target, fired on enemy infantry and trucks at Sidi Rezegh. On the afternoon of 6 December 1941, three guns of 3./FlaK-Regiment 33 supported II./Panzer-Regiment 8's attack on British forces on the height 3km from Bir el Gobi. FlaK B and its SdKfz 7 were knocked out by enemy artillery fire. (Library of Congress 01147v)

On 27 November 15.Panzer-Division, heading back towards Libya from the Egyptian border, was ambushed whilst driving through low land from nearby heights. The 3./FlaK 33 with them could not be brought into position initially because vehicles from the column were between them and the enemy. Eventually they could fire; however, at 1430hrs two German Me 110 aircraft appeared and bombs exploded near the guns. Panzer-Regiment 8 attacked, with the heavy FlaK formed into a firing line in support, despite the guns being in a vulnerable position. Although the situation was not propitious, the British retreated. Despite this reprieve, elsewhere two guns from

Indian troops examining a captured FlaK 18 established in a well dug-in position that would leave very little of the gun's structure exposed when engaging ground targets, Libya c.1942. On 7 December, 15.Panzer-Division was attacked from the south by enemy tanks in flat terrain with no cover. The guns were vulnerable, and the FlaK C crew were wounded by British artillery fire. The SdKfz 7 was able to extricate the FlaK C gun. On 13 December the battery had only a single operational gun because of losses to crews. (Bettmann/Getty Images)

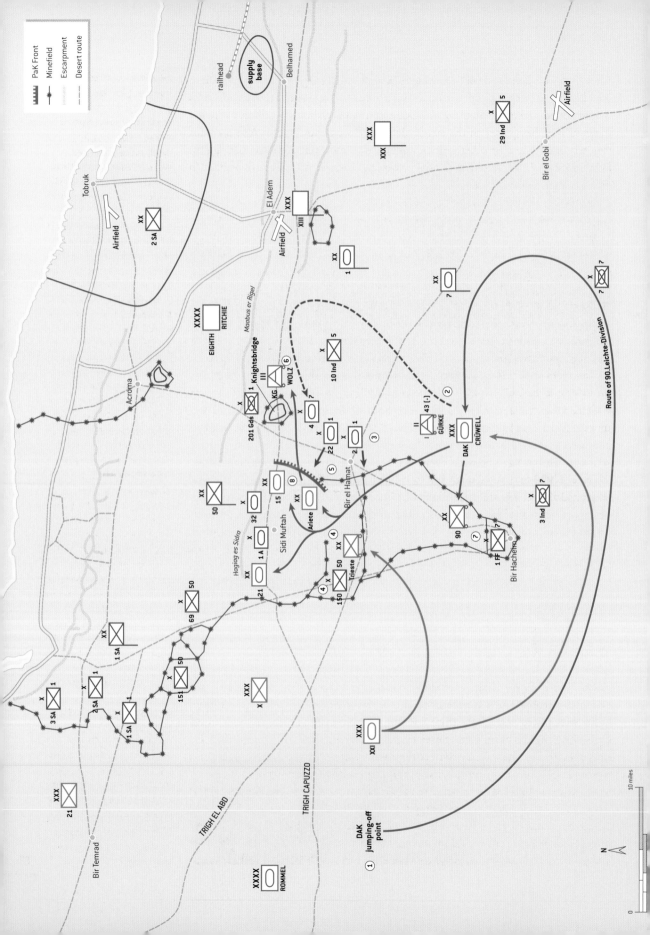

PaK Front
Minefield
Escarpment
Desert route

railhead

supply base

Belhamed

Tobruk

Airfield

2 SA XX

El Adem

Airfield

XXX XIII

XX 1

XX 7

XXX

29 Ind X 5

Airfield

Bir el Gobi

Acroma

Maabus er Rigel

EIGHTH XXXX
RITCHIE

Knightsbridge
III KG 1
WOLZ 6

201 Gds X

X 4 7

X 22 1

X 2 1

10 Ind X 5

5

II 43 (-)
GÜRKE
XXX
DAK
CRÜWELL

2

Hagiag es Sidra

50 XX

X 32

XX 15

XX Ariete

Sidi Muftah

Bir el Hamat

8

XX 90

7

XX 1A

XX 21

XX 50 Trieste

150 4

4

1 FF X 7

Bir Hacheim

3 Ind X 7

50 X 69

1 SA XX

151 X 50

XXX X

Bir Temrad

3 SA X 1

2 SA X 1

1 SA X 1

21 XXX

TRIGH EL ABD

TRIGH CAPUZZO

Route of 90.Leichte-Division

XXX XXI

XXXX ROMMEL

DAK
jumping-off
point

1

N

0   10 miles

3./FlaK 18 were destroyed whilst moving back with Aufklärungs-Abteilung 33 because they lacked infantry support. Crüwell issued rules that stipulated heavy FlaK guns should not be used in the front line without the cover of infantry, regardless of whether the guns were being used in the attack, defence or were moving out. Also the guns would be used only if no other weapon was available, they were not to be used against lightly armoured vehicles or guns, and they were to be moved only at speeds of 20km/h or less to prevent breakdowns.

Elsewhere, heavy losses prompted the release of 1. and 2./FlaK 33; however, 1./FlaK 33 was immobilized and 2./FlaK 33 surrounded in Halfaya Pass. On 30 November a single gun from 3./FlaK 33 and three guns from 8./FlaK 25 were hit by 20 bombers whilst in the open with their trucks not moved back. Three guns were lost. On 1 December Fromm was wounded near Belhamed; Hauptmann Haberland replaced him. By 4 December Rommel had only 40 tanks, while a replenished 7th Armoured Division had 140. In December a PAK front was established near Agedabia. Rommel, to support the Italians, brought forward the Reserve FlaK Abteilung with guns that did not have a gun shield despite the protests of Luftwaffe commanders. The unit was partially motorized. Orders specified the unit should engage targets only at long range.

Rommel's opponent in January 1942 was the untested armour from Britain. By then Rommel had 173 tanks. The nine guns available to I./FlaK 18, I./FlaK 33 and 6./FlaK 25 formed a mobile reserve when he began a new offensive that took him to the Gazala Line. At the end of the month I./FlaK 33, ordered to Tripoli, handed its guns to I./FlaK 18; the two batteries of I./FlaK 33 at Halfaya, out of supplies, had to surrender. In February I./FlaK 18 with seven heavy FlaK guns supported Rommel's advance. The reserve Abteilung went to Benghazi with 6./FlaK 25 where they found usable munitions still present. Rommel refused to let FlaK-Regiment 102 have new heavy FlaK guns promised them; instead he made sure they went to I./FlaK 18 to, as he put it, shoot tanks rather than holes in the sky. By April I./FlaK 18 had 12 guns. Marwan-Schlosser reported that the new I./FlaK 43 was short on trucks; the Luftwaffe kept its transport column. Trucks had to prioritize ammunition rather than general supplies. The 1./FlaK 43 was assigned to Rommel's DAK Kampfstaffel.

GAZALA

Auchinleck was told to prepare for his offensive in May. British dispositions when Rommel's attack began were therefore farther forward and not suited to a defence. Stores were placed close to the front line and their protection influenced operational decisions. Brigade boxes were closer to the enemy line than they needed to be, extending to Bir Hacheim to protect the supplies at Belhamed. Once intelligence reports suggested an enemy offensive was in the offing, the British developed a defensive mentality. A static rather than mobile defence was used, based on the brigade rather than the division. Supporting guns were divided amongst the brigades. Six armoured and two motorized brigades were in reserve; however, the motorized brigades in hastily built positions on the left flank sent their trucks away. The disagreement about where Rommel would use his panzers prompted dispersal of their

OPPOSITE
Battle of Gazala, 26 May to 13 June 1942
1. Night 26/27 May 1942: Rommel moves around the Gazala Line with the DAK and Italian armoured units.
2. 27 May: British 4th Armoured Brigade attacks 15.Panzer-Division of the DAK, and Rommel orders Wolz to organize three batteries of I./FlaK 43 in a line to stop their advance. The 5th Royal Tank Regiment loses about 24 Grants, most to the heavy FlaK guns.
3. 28 May: 10th Hussars and 9th Lancers from British 2nd Armoured Brigade advance towards Bir el Hamat. The Crusaders of A Squadron, 10th Hussars on the flank attack 3./FlaK 43. The squadron is wiped out.
4. 30 May to 1 June: Rommel focuses on the isolated British 150th Brigade on the Gazala Line, and forces it to surrender.
5. 4–5 June: The British attack Rommel in the Cauldron with 22nd Armoured Brigade supported by 10th Indian Infantry Brigade. The Germans pull back their gun line prior to the supporting artillery bombardment, and target the British armour, effectively wiping out the 2nd Royal Gloucestershire Hussars. The 32nd Army Tank Brigade advances on Sidra Ridge without infantry support, and is targeted by AT guns when stuck in a minefield.
6. 6 June: Wolz, with 6. and 8./FlaK 25 and supporting units, attempts to block British units in the Knightsbridge Box.
7. 8–10 June: Wolz does not support Rommel at Bir Hacheim, captured by 90.Leichte-Division.
8. 12–13 June: British armoured brigades fail to break through the German line. The Gazala Line is abandoned by the British.

A crewman photographed abandoning his Valentine Mk III and surrendering after the vehicle caught fire as a result of suffering a direct hit from Italian artillery or AT guns, Libya, April 1942. Though made in great numbers, more reliable than the Crusader and popular enough with its crews, the Valentine was not the tank that the British really needed, having only moderate armour and the same 2-pdr that by mid-1942 was obsolescent at best. Later models were upgraded to carry the 6-pdr, but the tank's basic design originated in prewar thinking, hampering its usefulness as a mid- or late-war battle tank. (Ullstein Bild via Getty Images)

armour; the presumption was they would not be able to gather in time to oppose Rommel's armoured divisions when their movements were known. Most brigade commanders thought a southern offensive was unlikely; however, Rommel would not attack in the middle of the British line because of the minefields.

To the north of Bir Hacheim was 4th Armoured Brigade, followed by 22nd Armoured Brigade by the minefield south of Bir el Hamat, and then 2nd Armoured Brigade east of them in reserve. The 201st Guards Brigade was next at Knightsbridge followed by 50th Infantry Division. The 2nd Royal Gloucestershire Hussars faced south to support 4th Armoured Brigade. In the evening of 26 May the notice that the panzer divisions had moved was given to the officers. The British outnumbered the Germans 3:2 in armour; Rommel, on a night move south of Bir Hacheim, thought the British had 650 tanks, only 20 per cent higher than his total. On 27 May, in the morning, he dispersed 3rd Indian Motorized Brigade and 7th Motorized Brigade. The British were taken by surprise and could launch their armour only in individual brigades. Initially 4th Armoured Brigade was encountered; their Grants exacted a high price on the German armour prior to moving back. The 22nd Armoured Brigade did not do as well, moving forward with little situational awareness and losing 30 tanks. The 2nd Armoured Brigade then advanced in the afternoon into the German flank, forcing them to falter – 9th Lancer's B Squadron Grants and E Battery Royal Horse Artillery supported the regiment's two Crusader squadrons moving forward, destroying 90.Leichte-Division's AT screen. Four heavy FlaK guns were apparently included in the haul. The Germans, with their supply lines exposed, had lost at least a third of their tanks.

The heavy FlaK guns were integral to pushing back 4th Armoured Brigade on 27 May. When 15.Panzer-Division encountered the Grants of 4th Armoured Brigade, the German tanks stood little chance. FlaK 43 guns nearby were widely dispersed moving in terrain without cover, as the order was to get ahead. The guns were firing limbered when targets presented themselves; however, the supply trucks were soon making haste to retreat and encountered Generalleutnant Walther Nehring with the commander of FlaK-Regiment 135, Wolz. They found Rommel's AOK Afrika Kampfstaffel at 1600hrs, which had 3./FlaK 43 attached. Rommel accused Wolz of creating a mess because he did not use his guns immediately. Nehring told Wolz to place his guns in a firing position 150m from each other and soon, emerging from a thick cloud of dust, 30–35 enemy tanks of 4th Armoured Brigade were seen 1,500m distant. The guns fired and soon the British decided to retreat. Major Ernst Gürke's 2./FlaK 43 then arrived; his guns were positioned 600m distant from 1./FlaK 43; 3./FlaK 43 followed half an hour later and was positioned on the opposite side. Three batteries on a front of 3,000m fired at enemy tanks 1,200m distant. The 3./FlaK 43 deployed four heavy guns pointing north-east and two south-east. The guns opened fire; six tanks were hit by the four guns pointing north-east. Then the British armour with artillery support attacked the two guns pointing south-east; three British tanks were quickly knocked out. By dusk the battery had taken a heavy toll, with 24 tanks, mostly Grants from 5th Royal Tank Regiment, destroyed. Despite the losses to the tank force, the British artillery continued to shell, forcing the battery to abandon its position in the late afternoon, moving back 900m and then in early evening 10km to the south-west of Bir el Hamrad.

Rommel was not strong enough to advance to the sea to complete the encirclement of the Gazala Line. His tanks would not receive supplies and would be south of Acroma on 28 and 29 May, unable to properly fight. Rommel was in a valley and relied on the FlaK guns to protect him. He needed to be defensive and thought the British would launch attacks. He would renew his attack when they had suffered losses. Marwan-Schlosser was unsure where enemy forces were and considered the

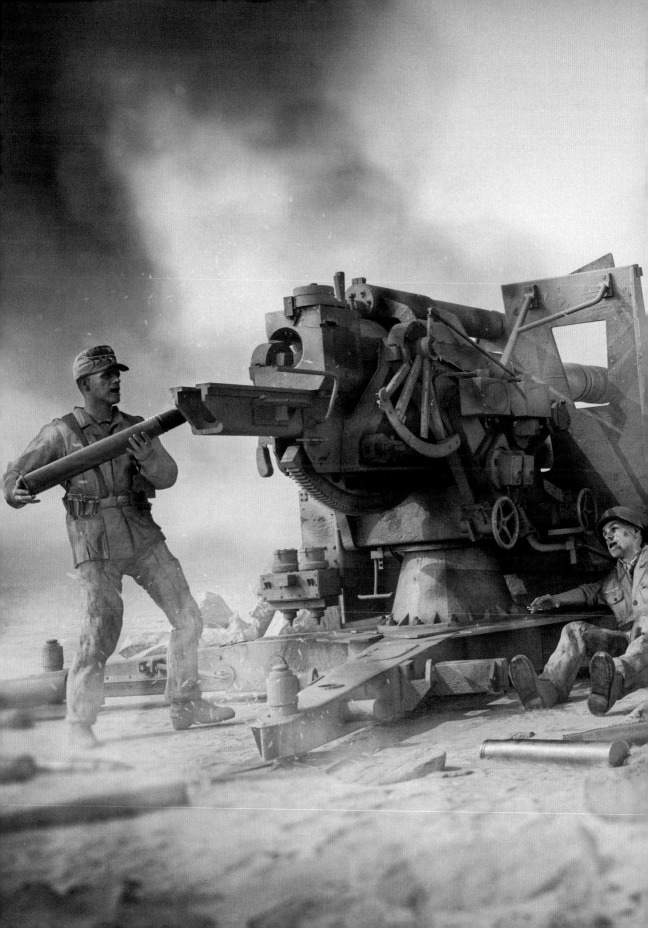

situation critical because his guns were lacking ammunition. He hoped the ammunition trucks would arrive before sunrise. On 28 May the British had an opportunity to assault a dispersed German force in isolated positions. In the afternoon they attacked the Italian armour holding Bir el Hamat with 1st Army Tank Brigade, and 2nd and 4th Armoured brigades.

On 28 May four guns of 3./FlaK 43 occupied a height and obtained good all-round observation; two guns advanced north-east towards an enemy tank force. At 0600hrs two guns from the height joined them. Soon British tanks fired on the two forward guns at 3,650m; however, when the heavy guns replied, they soon retreated. At 0715hrs the battery was ordered to join the Italians, though were soon pulled back to join the HQ to repel what appeared to be a suspected tank force that was massing in the north-east. Two FlaK guns from a different battery, a 5cm AT gun platoon, and three 2cm light FlaK guns joined them. The 5cm guns covered the deployment of the FlaK guns and were slightly in advance. An observation position was established on a height 2km to the north-east to give warning.

On the morning of 28 May, 2nd Armoured Brigade's 10th Hussars headed south and the C Squadron Grants suffered heavily when they shelled gun tractors belonging to heavy FlaK units. Then B Squadron's Crusaders with three troops (totalling ten tanks) moved on the German AT gun line, probably of 5cm guns, following a Royal Horse Artillery bombardment that laid down a smokescreen and also peppered the AT gun crews with HE; this first wave machine-gunned its way through the gun position; another five tanks, ordered to tow the guns away, were unable to attach ropes and instead destroyed three of them by placing hand grenades in the barrels.

In the afternoon of that day the 9th Lancers and its sister regiment the 10th Hussars were ordered to force Rommel onto the minefields. The 10th Hussars A Squadron was on the left and had to swing round as the brigade veered to the right; the squadron found itself going wider and deeper into the enemy's position than intended. The 3./FlaK 43 reported at 1815hrs a sudden attack by 15–20 Crusaders; some had gone round to the south-east (this was A Squadron). In 20 minutes, 13 were knocked out. Three that had attacked from the south-east were knocked out within the battery position at less than 50m. Two officers and six rank and file were captured. The squadron commander, Major R. Archer-Shee, told the German crews he mistook the battery for 5cm guns because of their low profile. A Zugkraftwagen was destroyed in the engagement. The Kampfstaffel had scattered during the attack. Rommel drove back to meet supply trucks, guiding them through the minefields. Fuel and ammunition restored the panzer divisions' striking power and mobility. Rommel kept them in a defensive position, with minefields guarding his western flank and guns his eastern flank. He would provoke British tanks to assault his defences whilst consolidating his position and dismantling the boxes.

On 29 May, in the early hours, British forces were detected to the north and 3./FlaK 43 was moved to a position 900m east of Bir el Hamat. Artillery fire compelled them to move 900m to the south-west. Reconnaissance found a British force moving from the north and north-east. The reinforced battery moved forward 900m to engage them. The Kampfstaffel advanced three tanks to distract the British in order to allow the battery to complete its deployment without interference. At 0830hrs the British were seen advancing. The enemy tanks opened fire at 1,800m with artillery helping

Gazala, 28 May 1942. At the height of a British armoured assault in the early days of the Battle of Gazala a FlaK 36 battery position has been overrun. Despite having taken heavy casualties, a small number of Crusader II tanks have penetrated the German line and are manoeuvring around the battery guns, attacking them from all directions and scattering their crews. One particularly aggressive tank has killed or chased away most of one FlaK 36's crew, driving over one of its outriggers. One Kanonier, protected by the gun's tough structure, is attempting to get up, scraped, bruised and shaken but otherwise unhurt, whilst a second crewman – a sweat-stained Gefreiter in a weather-beaten tropical cap – has aimed the gun at the retreating British Crusader and fired, hitting it at a range of 40m. The tank's turret is blown off in a cloud of flame and inky black smoke whilst the Gefreiter grabs another Pzgr. 39 shell, ready to continue the fight.

A column of Grant tanks of 5th Royal Tank Regiment on the move in the Western Desert, 17 February 1942. On 2 June 1942, 2nd Royal Gloucestershire Hussars refitted with a squadron of Grants and two of M3s from 4th Hussars. H Squadron formed a column with a battery from the Royal Horse Artillery, a company of infantry and some 6-pdr guns in order to raid German supply lines for the next two weeks, and in July fought on the El Alamein position. G Squadron was in reserve on the Cairo road. F and H squadrons would be with 5th Royal Tank Regiment at Alam el Halfa. The squadrons then went to join other regiments when 2nd Royal Gloucestershire Hussars disbanded. (Capt. G. Keating/ Imperial War Museums via Getty Images)

them. The tanks would advance no closer and the battery fired and five were destroyed. A truck loaded with ammunition exploded, a panzer in the battery position was knocked out; one heavy gun was damaged by a hit on the air cylinder on the breech, wounding Leutnant Maiwald, and completely knocked out by a hit on the breech itself. Three men were seriously wounded, two men lightly wounded, and 117 rounds were used against the tanks. An inspection later in the day would identify them as Matildas. A distance of 275m south of Bir el Hamat, ten Hurricanes engaged them, and the 2cm drove them off. Rommel then took the Kampfstaffel 8km north-north-west. The battery guarded the flank. Rommel made a reconnaissance and then moved on 6km with his Kampfstaffel. No British forces were seen, and two guns deployed on a height to the north-east.

At 0200hrs on 30 May a night march was completed by 3./FlaK 43 and the Kampfstaffel to Bir et Tamar. In the morning the battery was 5km north of this position; six guns pointed east and two north-west. A radio-equipped armoured car and radio-equipped armoured half-track were given to the battery. The battery OP reported targets with the radio at 6km distance. The British force was effectively engaged. At 1430hrs two guns were pushed forward to the north and were fired at by artillery, causing four casualties. At 1600hrs this fire became intense and the battery moved 3km north-west of Bir et Tamar; however, no further attacks materialized. Then, on 1 June, 150th Brigade, Rommel's initial target, was destroyed. The route for his Axis supply columns was clear.

On 4 June the British attacked Rommel in the Cauldron with 400 tanks; Rommel had 230 German and Italian AFVs. The British attempted to use combined arms tactics on 5 June with infantry initially attacking; however, the artillery barrage fell on empty desert because the Germans had pulled back. On 5 June, following a barrage,

A Crusader I or II burns after taking a direct hit, one of the unfortunate vehicle's crew crawling to safety in the foreground. On 30 May 1942 Rommel formed defensive positions on the reverse slope of a crest. Derelict tanks were used as bait on the ridge. Heavy FlaK hit the 9th Lancers when the ridge was reached. CS cruisers fired smoke to cover the retreat. Lumsden told the regiment to charge again with the support of artillery firing smoke at 1520hrs. The guns fired at 1510hrs, but the smoke had dissipated by the time the regiment, with two squadrons from 22nd Armoured Brigade in support, reached the ridge. By the end of May, of the 9th Lancers' 47 tanks, 32 were lost, including 18 beyond local repair, and there were 62 casualties. In the aftermath two squadrons received new tanks near Capuzzo on 14 June, and C Squadron was sent to Egypt. (Eric Borchert/Ullstein Bild via Getty Images)

22nd Armoured Brigade advanced on a ridge east of Bir el Hamat. Indian infantry were supposed to have captured the enemy gun positions early that morning; however, the guns had already pulled out to the second ridge. 2nd Royal Gloucestershire Hussars slowly climbed the gradual slope to the second ridge, and the enemy guns opened fire. They were saved from complete disaster because the Germans opened at long range, firing into the sun and the mirage; British field guns caused smoke and dust to further obscure them. The 2nd Royal Gloucestershire Hussars could see no targets and had to retire to their gun line. The brigade lost 70 tanks. On 6 June, 2nd Royal Gloucestershire Hussars was targeted by heavy FlaK. Lieutenant-Colonel Birley's tank was hit. The 2nd Royal Gloucestershire Hussars was sent to refit, except for H Squadron, which was sent to 7th Motor Brigade near Bir Hacheim. In total 82 casualties were suffered in 16 days. Still the British had 330 tanks and the Germans and Italians 230.

On 5 June Rommel had ordered Wolz to group 6., 8., and 9./FlaK 25 with Aufklärungs-Abteilung 33 and 1./Panzerjäger 33. These units moved north-east to block the Trigh Capuzzo to stop the British retreating. At the same time, the panzer divisions were to attack eastwards to push the British onto the guns. At 1830hrs British tanks were fired upon by heavy FlaK heading eastwards. At night Wolz was worried the tanks could retreat past his guns, and he brought the reconnaissance vehicles to where the guns were located and kept the crews awake during the night ready to fire. On the morning of 6 June a mass of vehicles was seen 50m below the guns in a valley. Artillery fire was brought down on the heavy FlaK from a British observer close by. Wolz's guns unknowingly were in the Knightsbridge box. He moved his guns facing north to face east; 40 tanks were approaching. The British moved south to approach from a flank and Wolz moved his guns to form a gun line to target them. Ammunition was scarce by the end of the day, when 3./FlaK 43 arrived; 14 British tanks were knocked out.

With the dark, KG Wolz was ordered to Bir el Hamat to resupply. Rommel arrived on 7 June at 1715hrs and took Aufklärungs-Abteilung 33 from Wolz. The latter was ordered to move at night to 6km north of Bir Hacheim with two companies of engineers and tanks of Kampfstaffel Kiehl. He was to attack the position through a minefield, led by Rommel himself at 0600hrs on 8 June. Wolz that morning found no Stukas to support the attack, and a company of grenadiers promised him had also not arrived. Marwan-Schlosser persuaded Wolz to stop the attack. British aircraft had already destroyed a gun and damaged another. Rommel instead led 90.Leichte-Division against the Free French on 8 June, forcing them to retreat on the night of 10 June.

On 12 and 13 June the British armour counterattacked Rommel's force a last time. The British lost 138 tanks. The Gazala Line could not be supported and the surviving British brigades began to retreat. The 2nd Armoured Brigade was on Sidi Rezegh Ridge on 17 June with two field batteries and 16 guns of AT units in support. When about 40 German tanks appeared on the ridge opposite and began to approach, the British guns limbered and retreated. The 9th Lancer's B Squadron's Grants were being hit and were ordered to reverse back from the ridge and then, when they had covered a mile, to fire smoke. Heavy FlaK on the ridge helped German tanks engage the regiment. Only a single Grant was operational at the end of the battle.

AFTER GAZALA

Marwan-Schlosser wrote to Rommel that the latter's view of the guns as essential to the DAK was in jeopardy as, within two weeks, out of 46 guns, six were destroyed, eight heavily damaged, with many only partially working. In early June, 21.Panzer-Division had 1. and 3.Batterie of I./FlaK 18; 15.Panzer-Division had 1. and 2./FlaK 43; and 90.Leichte-Division had 1/.FlaK 6 plus 2./FlaK 18; 6. and 8.Batterie of II./FlaK 25 were with Aufklärungs-Abteilung 33. The 7./FlaK 25 could be used only against planes because of a lack of trucks. FlaK 25 was missing a lot of trucks due to the battles around Knightsbridge. The 3./FlaK 43 was with the Kampfstaffel. On 22 June, 7./FlaK 25 and 2./FlaK 6 were used on aerial targets at El Adem. Wolz asked Generalmajor Burchhardt, Kommandierender General des Luftgaues zvB Afrika, for some carriages because many were broken; 6. and 8./FlaK 25 were in Bardia to have carriages repaired.

The British wanted to hold Sollum on the frontier; however, a retreat to Mersa Matruh was deemed necessary. Rommel had only 45 Panzer IIIs and Panzer IVs. The armour the British had amounted to 159. Rommel sought to flank the British positions at Mersa Matruh. The British tanks were to the south. On 27 June, 90.Leichte-Division was on the road east of Mersa Matruh after moving through

A tank commander in his new M3 Grant, Libya, May or June 1942. In early 1942 Auchinleck gave each armoured division (1st and 7th) a single armoured brigade and infantry brigade. On 8 February Gott tried a new establishment for the armoured brigade. The 2nd Armoured Brigade would have a regiment of armoured cars, two armoured regiments, 24 field guns, 16 AT guns and a battalion of infantry. In early April new tanks acquired by 9th Lancers gave A Squadron 16 Crusaders, B Squadron 23 M3s and two cruisers and C Squadron three Crusaders, eight M3s and a cruiser. The HQ Squadron had two each of Crusaders and M3s. By 22 May, when the Grants arrived, B Squadron had 13 Grants, a Crusader and two M3s; A Squadron and C Squadron had 16 Crusaders each. (IPC Magazines/Picture Post/Hulton Archive/Getty Images)

the weakened British position to the south of the town. The 6. and 8./FlaK 25 joined Wolz from Bardia on 28 June. Wolz was between the besieged forces and those attempting their relief. The 9.Batterie, with 2cm guns, helped provide protection from infantry. In front, the slope of Raqabet el Sika went down to the valley. The FlaK was not able to fire down and Wolz had to move the guns back from the ridge. The armour did not counterattack and instead retreated. British vehicles moved in mass at night and cleared the ridge, driving through the gun positions, although some were hit. Major Dittrich, the FlaK 25 commander, was wounded and Marwan-Schlosser took his position. The Indians in Mersa Matruh had to break out and suffered heavy losses.

Rommel reached El Alamein on 1 July. Here the British had two closed flanks. The Ruweisat Ridge 16km south of El Alamein dominated the surrounding terrain. German intelligence had failed to determine the locations of the boxes. Infiltration was not achieved. The 25-pdrs stopped 90.Leichte-Division from moving around the South African Division box. Nehring took the decision to eliminate the Deir el Shein box occupied by Indian infantry; however, losses reduced German armour to 37. On 1 July, 8./FlaK 25, with Kampfstaffel Kiehl, was ominously targeted by artillery and planes. Rommel moved the DAK against the South Africans on 2 July. Auchinleck gathered his tanks east of Ruweisat Ridge. Field guns interdicted the DAK on their approach to the box. On 3 July Rommel reached the ridge. On 1 July B Squadron, 9th Lancers had sent 12 Grants and four Crusaders to its eastern end. The Germans were on the opposite end, unable to throw the British off the ridge.

A 25-pdr of the Royal Artillery engaging German targets in July 1942. When the British used their Ordnance QF 25-pdr (88x292mm R shell) field guns on enemy armour, their HE shells could cause devastating damage. They were also supplied a limited number of AP (later APBC) shot. However, with a lower muzzle velocity of only 518m/s when firing HE, hitting a fast-moving vehicle proved hard, though their circular firing platform offered rapid traverse. (Daily Mirror/ Mirrorpix via Getty Images)

On 22 July B Squadron, 9th Lancers, with Grants, had orders to advance through the minefield in the area of Ruweisat Ridge and clear the enemy from a depression on the north side. At 1,400m Lieutenant Mostyn's tank was hit by heavy FlaK. Sergeant Collier fired at the gun with his 75mm – he had a good bracket and ordered further corrections; then a shell from the heavy FlaK gun hit the barrel of his 75mm. The turret-mounted 37mm took up the job of firing at the FlaK gun, but malfunctioned. Mostyn's tank quickly laid down a smokescreen and reversed to safety, despite a burning Grant partially blocking the lane. Five Grants were destroyed and seven damaged.

In late July in the north 7./FlaK 25 and 3./FlaK 43 were on aerial duty; 1./FlaK 43 was in repair in El Daba; 6./FlaK 25 was on airfield duty; 1. and 2./FlaK 18 needed replenishment and were also on airfield duty; 2./FlaK 43 was with 15.Panzer-Division; 21.Panzer-Division had 3./FlaK 18; 90.Leichte-Division had 1./FlaK 6; and 2./FlaK 6 was with Aufklärungs-Abteilung 580. On 3 July Wolz moved 7./FlaK 25 and 3./FlaK 43 south to combat British tanks near Italian positions on Djebel Ridge with the help of 15.Panzer-Division. Marwan-Schlosser rejoined the staff when he was wounded. On 5 July Wolz and Marwan-Schlosser were near the front line, Marwan-Schlosser having to relieve a Leutnant when he was unable to move his two heavy and two 2cm guns forward. The officer was moved back to the airfield.

The 3./FlaK 6 was brought forward, as 1./FlaK 6 (with 15.Panzer-Division) only had three guns. KG Wolz, now with 2./FlaK 18, was given 2./FlaK 53, and 3./FlaK 53 went to 90.Leichte-Division. The 1./FlaK 53 was with Wolz's regimental HQ; 8./FlaK 25 was in refit; 1./FlaK 43 was with the DAK HQ; and 3./FlaK 43 with the AOK Kampfstaffel. In total 38 heavy FlaK guns could support the Alam el Halfa operation; their scope was limited because Rommel's armoured columns were caught in minefields. During the night, aircraft would target the heavy FlaK guns; because of missing searchlights and radar, the planes could not be targeted. Rommel decided to move back; however, on the night of 2/3 September planes targeted 2./FlaK 18 and 1./FlaK 43, destroying both batteries. The 7./FlaK 25, in an Italian base, fought off a British counterattack; 8./FlaK 53 was temporarily surrounded; and 3./FlaK 33 arrived with Funkmessgerät used for early warning, searchlight direction or gun laying, and local observation and tracking.

Montgomery prepared his next offensive carefully, giving both sides some time to replenish. On the night of 23/24 October, 2nd Armoured Brigade attacked during the beginning of El Alamein. Two tank regiments supported two infantry battalions in their advance to Kidney Ridge. Mines were not completely cleared when, in the daylight, the Germans used their heavy FlaK; however, losses were light with only seven tanks lost in the brigade, as German crews were firing into the sun. The 9th Lancers in reserve could not initially spot the guns. As the day advanced, the light improved and two heavy FlaK guns were hit. When friendly bombers appeared, the heavy FlaK targeted them by raising their barrels, and the British could see the guns. At 1700hrs on 25 October the Shermans of C Squadron, 10th Hussars, following a bombardment by five artillery batteries, moved on a ridge; when the smoke cleared from the bombardment, the squadron lost five vehicles to heavy FlaK guns, and the remainder withdrew. C Squadron handed its five remaining tanks to A Squadron and departed to refit. B Squadron, with Crusader IIIs, did not have the range to target the heavy FlaK. By comparison, a Sherman knocked out a heavy FlaK gun from a crest when a mortar crew spotted the gun.

The heavy FlaK was holding and three night attacks on them by infantry on 25–27 October failed to completely clear them; however, Shermans using their indirect fire from crest lines successfully targeted two heavy FlaK guns. By dawn on 28 October, 9th Lancers were near the ridge and enemy armour was readying to counterattack. A Squadron charged to the north-west on flat ground, causing some damage to enemy infantry and their support weapons. Whilst smoke was used on the heavy FlaK, other tanks moved to the crest, from where they observed 30 enemy tanks and started firing; however, no breakthrough was made and 2nd Armoured Brigade was brought out of the line. The 24th Armoured Brigade occupied their position; they charged the ridge with heavy loss, ignoring the warnings of the departing unit. The unit was disbanded and the Shermans went to 10th Hussars. On 2 November, 9th Lancers with 2nd Armoured Brigade took part in Operation *Supercharge* in support of the 2nd New Zealand Division. German reserves were by then exhausted. On 4 November the DAK was in retreat. The heavy FlaK guns would be vulnerable during the withdrawal. On 5 November the reconnaissance troop of 10th Hussars captured a heavy FlaK gun being limbered; however, another gun ambushed the armoured cars and escaped.

Rommel was able to bring most of his army out of Libya and occupy defences on the Mareth Line on the Tunisian–Libyan border. The German defenders on hills that offered good observation looked at low-lying ground with AT ditches, emplacements and minefields. A frontal attack in March 1943 by infantry with 2nd Armoured

Brigade, supported by a flank move by the NZ formations at Gabès on the southern end of the line, offered the prospect of success; however, when 50th Division could not move its AT guns forward and was counterattacked by German armour, 2nd Armoured Brigade, sent to follow the New Zealanders across terrain that included soft sand, was not available to them. On 25 March the Germans in the south were holding the valley near El Hamma. The next day 2nd Armoured Brigade was able to advance at 1600hrs. The going was rough and hilly. Clear lines in the minefield were followed. The infantry were 730m in front of the brigade. A fog limited lines of sight. In the evening the advance continued in the moonlight. A heavy FlaK gun 8km from El Hamma started firing, knocking out a Sherman. A Sherman from B Squadron, 9th Lancers, approaching to within 100m, drove through the gun position, firing. Although the village could not be captured until two days later, the Germans were encouraged to retreat from Gabès as 2nd Armoured Brigade was in place to cut the German supply route to the Mareth Line; however, on 27 March Wolz at El Hamma still had time to form a FlaK position that knocked out 14 tanks.

On 9 April Wolz, with I./FlaK 33, was on Chebkat el Hassane, in southern Tunisia. On the ridge Wolz positioned 3.Batterie towards the hill at Erlet el Hamra; 1.Batterie was by the road to Mahares by the sea, and 2.Batterie in-between them. At 1000hrs tanks were seen near Erlet el Hamra. In addition 50 tanks, probably from 8th Armoured Brigade, were taking cover in olive plantations. A battalion of 164.Leichte-Division was slowly being wiped out. The commander, Major Richter, was ordered by Wolz to move to a high point that looked down upon the road junction whilst his guns stopped the tanks, destroying three. The 164.Leichte-Division then ordered Wolz to move his guns back 4km. This proved difficult in the terrain, whilst the infantry could move rapidly. Wolz moved his guns into position to cover tanks from 15.Panzer-Division approaching. He enabled the tanks to counterattack, and the British breakthrough to the Sfax road was foiled. Wolz was awarded the Ritterkreuz.

The Hermann Göring Division transferred from southern France to Tunisia in late 1942 with six batteries of heavy FlaK. On 22 April 1943, 2./FlaK-Regiment Hermann Göring (HG) with a 2cm gun, two MGs and two FlaK 36 positioned next to 3./FlaK-Regiment HG. One gun was 400m south of the road; a second gun was 740m south and back from the front. These guns were observed by the British on heights 2–3km from the guns. In total 100 British tanks were amongst the heights, and closed in on the guns at 1800hrs; however, they were difficult to see. The next morning, at 0600hrs, 20 to 25 tanks cleared a ridge to the right of the road. Two were knocked out by 3./FlaK HG. The tanks remained hull down, firing from a gully. German panzers counterattacked with limited results. The British fired smoke shells throughout the encounter. At 0940hrs six tanks advanced from the gully against the gun from 2./FlaK HG. Five shots at 450m immobilized one tank and set two others on fire. The surviving tank fired at the gun and destroyed it. Another 20 minutes later British tanks moved through the heights, and the second gun of 2./FlaK HG immobilized two and set two on fire with seven shots at 1,100m. As the crew targeted the next tank, the gun was hit and destroyed when the cylinder exploded. The 2cm gun was ordered destroyed and the surviving crew retreated.

On 14 April, 1st Armoured Division moved to join First Army in the final battle for Tunisia launched on the night of 22/23 April. B Squadron, 9th Lancers was ambushed by heavy FlaK clearing a gully in the Goubellat Valley, and 10th Hussars deployed to the head of the valley to help. In early May the brigade was at the entrance of Creteville Pass, between Hammam Lif outside Tunis and Hammamet on the east coast. The British were attacking east from Hammam Lif – 9th Lancers supported 7th Motor Brigade assaulting the pass. On 7 May C Squadron entered the pass. Heavy FlaK guns were sited to fire down the road with plentiful ammunition. Two officers from the Hermann Göring Division had already stated they wanted to surrender because they were out of ammunition. C Squadron began to descend the other side past a roadblock with ammunition stacked beside the guns. B Squadron passed through down a valley. About 1.5km in lay a village with a large factory with heavy FlaK fire coming from it. Another valley went farther east, and from here German tanks appeared. The heavy FlaK was picked off slowly. By 9 May the village was empty and German soldiers were ready to surrender by the road a little farther on. A battery of heavy FlaK was seen abandoned.

THE AMERICAN EXPERIENCE IN TUNISIA

At the start of the Tunisian campaign Major-General Ward's 1st Armored Division was a powerful and extremely well-equipped force, though like the British before them the ratio of tanks to infantry in the American armoured forces was unbalanced in favour of armour – six armoured battalions to only three armoured infantry and three field artillery battalions (Calhoun 2003, p. 38). One of the most significant advantages that the force enjoyed was the quality of its armour; the M3 light tank was a proven design and the medium M3s and M4s, though not without shortcomings, had acquitted themselves well with the British in the North African campaigns of 1942, and were a match for the Panzer III and IV (the Tiger having yet to make its debut). The main issues facing American tank crews were doctrine, training and experience.

Doctrine was based on prewar ideas about tanks as a highly mobile striking force that would conduct operations against an enemy's rear areas. It seems little attention was paid to the practical lessons learned by the British in North Africa. The tactics for tank combat as laid out in the March 1942 Armored Force Field Manual appeared sensible enough in the main, but aside from noting the role of the support force (mortars, artillery and infantry) in the armoured advance, there was relatively little focus on well-balanced combined arms operations. More concerning was the role allotted to armoured units: the primary purpose of the light tank was 'to close with the enemy and to disrupt the hostile organization in vital rear areas by fast, bold action', whilst for the medium tanks the key objective was 'to assist the attack of the light tank units, chiefly by neutralizing or destroying the hostile anti-tank weapons. When organized resistance is encountered, especially anti-tank guns, medium tank units will usually precede the light tank units for this purpose' (FM 17–10 1942, p. 46). Medium tanks also had a secondary role in defending the light tanks from enemy armour, but the tank destroyer battalions were considered the prime tool in combating panzer forces. Little of this doctrine would survive unchanged after battle was joined.

An M3 of the US 1st Armored Division driving through thick mud, most likely around the area of Sened Station, in Tunisia, early February 1943. Note the MG turret atop the 37mm gun (housing a .30-cal. M1919A4), a feature that the British dispensed with on their versions of the vehicle. The US 1st Armored Division was supposed to be entirely outfitted with M4s, but the desperate straits of the British armoured forces in the bleak days after Gazala saw large numbers of the new tanks dispatched to the Eighth Army, resulting in the M3 remaining in several of the division's battalions for the battle at Sidi Bou Zid on 14–15 February 1943. (Eliot Elisofon/The LIFE Picture Collection via Getty Images)

On 10 July 1940 the activation of the Armored Force took place, with 1st Armored Division activated five days later. The Armored Force developed rapidly, expanding with the rest of the army, its more experienced units being stripped of men to form cadres around which new units could be raised. Training in the established doctrine aimed to generate a force of four armoured divisions, with 1st Armored Division, being the most senior, the first to be deployed overseas; it sailed for Ireland in April 1942 ahead of Operation *Torch*. The division's men were largely inexperienced, but that was inevitable in what was effectively a brand-new army. Most of them had undergone 13 weeks of basic training, after which, as future tankmen, they would attend the Armored Force School or Armored Force Replacement Training Center, receiving further training once they reached their units. This last aspect proved most beneficial for the men of 1st Armored, the division going to considerable effort to improve gunnery, coordination with artillery units and battlefield drills. The men developed a good knowledge of their vehicles, their capabilities and shortcomings, as well as how to operate them according to the existing ideas of movement and attack.

By the time they had deployed to Tunisia, the 1st Armored was still a relatively green outfit, having seen little combat in Algeria after the *Torch* landings. The instinct of American tank commanders was to use their mobility and firepower to take the fight to the enemy, even if that meant outstripping their supporting arms or friendly air power in the process. In some quarters there was a lack of professionalism, and there were many necessary skills that were still only half-learned, but it was a lack of training in how to engage enemy armour and AT defences that would prove to be most costly. There was little attention paid to such necessities in the existing doctrine, and the only way to learn would be through experience.

SIDI BOU ZID

In broad terms the German plan aimed to break through the Allied defences on the Eastern Dorsal Mountains and capture Sidi Bou Zid, from where they would strike westwards making either for Tébessa or Le Kef depending on the situation on the ground. The attack on Sidi Bou Zid, launched at dawn on 14 February 1942, was conducted by four Kampfgruppen, two (drawn from 10.Panzer-Division) attacking through the Faïd Pass to the north and two (from 21. Panzer-Division) coming up from the Maïzila Pass to the south, all converging on the town. Each Kampfgruppe was a combined arms force built around a panzer or panzergrenadier unit, with those of 10.Panzer-Division including two 8.8cm-equipped FlaKkampftruppen from Panzer-Artillerie-Regiment 90, and 21.Panzer Division having three 8.8cm-equipped FlaKkampftruppen likely supplied from DAK Luftwaffe units.

In Tunisia the 1st Armored Division's 202 M3/M4 medium tanks and 92 M3/M5 light tanks were organized into temporary combined arms task forces called 'combat commands', designated CCA through CCD. Of its four medium tank battalions, three had M4s or M4A1s, whilst 2/13th Armored Regiment had different types of 'Lees' that were replaced with M4/M4A1s as they broke down or were lost in action (Rottman 2008, p. 49). CCA and CCC were the task forces in the region of Sidi Bou Zid and Kasserine.

Lieutenant-Colonel Louis V. Hightower's armoured reaction force was the first to engage the advancing Germans, though it was quickly apparent that it could be little more than a delaying action. Stationed by Sidi Bou Zid, his force comprised M4s from H/1st Armored and I/1st Armored, as well as approximately 12 M3 GMCs from A/701st Tank Destroyer Battalion. His tank's radioman, Sergeant Clarence W. Coley, watched as Hightower's command was obliterated by enemy guns, 'including a lot of "Eighty-eights"' (Howe 1979, p. 151), though whether those were from FlaK guns, PzKpfw VIs or other guns can only be conjecture. There had been little attempt at manoeuvring by Hightower's force, or to adapt its tactics to engaging an enemy primarily made up of armour and AT guns. Recalling the experience for the education of other tankers, Hightower observed that in a tank battle the Germans would generally 'try to suck you into an anti-tank gun trap. Their light tanks will bait you in by playing around just outside effective range. When you start after them, they turn tail and draw you in within range of their 88-millimeter guns. First they open up on you with their guns in depth. Then when you try to flank them you find yourself under fire of carefully concealed guns at a shorter range. We've just got to learn to pick those guns up before closing in on them' (Calhoun 2003, p. 58). Of Hightower's 51 tanks, only seven survived, but worse was to follow.

In an attempt to remedy the situation and rescue the American infantry on hills around Sidi Bou Zid cut off by the German advance, Colonel Stack of CCC organized a counterattack. Setting out on 15 February, it was spearheaded by Lieutenant-Colonel James D. Alger's medium tanks of 2/1st Armored, with B/701st Tank Destroyer Battalion as well as that battalion's reconnaissance company on the flanks for support. The force was rounded out by the 1st Armored Division's M3 half-track-equipped 3/6th Armored Infantry, as well as two batteries of 105mm T19 self-propelled howitzers from 68th Field Artillery Batallion. The battlegroup moved out at 1240hrs, having conducted no serious reconnaissance but believing they were facing no more than 40–60 panzers (it was approximately double that number). As with Hightower the previous day, there was no consideration given to what particular tactics ought to be employed against AT gun screens or panzer forces.

The Germans quickly prepared an ambush; the American tanks would have to pass over three wadis that had few places where they could be crossed easily, and it was on the second of these wadi crossings that the German gun screen had been focused. As expected, the M4 tanks were advancing by company and bunched up as they navigated the deep wadis;

British troops pass an abandoned German SdKfz 8 and a spiked 8.8cm FlaK 41 on the Mareth Line, April 1943. Capable of firing shells at a higher velocity than the FlaK 18/36/37, the FlaK 41 L/74 was overly complex and difficult to use and maintain in the field. A small contingent of these guns, mounted on trailers with distinctive gunshields and towed by the SdKfz 8 because of the gun's greater weight, were dispatched to North Africa towards the end of 1942, but their impact on the campaign was negligible. As a result, future deployments of the system were almost exclusively within Germany in the AA role. (AirSeaLand Photos, 144223)

D/1 had passed through the second wadi and was fanning out in an inverted 'V' formation while the following F/1 was still at the chokepoint when two 4.7cm guns and four 8.8cm FlaK guns hidden in olive groves on the south-eastern flank opened up at 1540hrs, immediately destroying several of F/1's vehicles. The Americans returned fire at once, only for D/1 to find itself attacked by strong panzer forces on both flanks. The Americans fought back hard, overrunning several of the 10.Panzer-Division's heavy FlaK positions and destroying at least four, perhaps five 8.8cm guns, but their invidious position and the weight of enemy forces told against them; by 1740hrs it was all over. Only the four US tanks that had been held in reserve, most of the self-propelled artillery, and the 3/6th Armored Infantry had survived – the remaining 52 tanks of Alger's battalion were wrecked, abandoned or burning.

The German assault that had started so well soon petered out in the face of logistical realities and a renewed sense of determination among the defending Allied forces. Within little more than a month the roles were exchanged, with US forces pushing eastwards through Maknassy and El Guettar in an attempt to pierce the German positions on the Gabès Road and link up with Montgomery's forces, who had just broken through the Mareth Line. The efforts of several of 1st Armored Division's tank battalions were blunted again on 30–31 March by ferocious German AT screens supported by air attacks, but the tide had turned decisively, and by mid-April the division was regrouping and preparing for the final push on Tunis. US armoured units had suffered significant losses but had been able to rebound and take the fight to the enemy. Many of the reasons for their failures can be attributed to issues of command and control, as well as the habit of widely dispersing a division's units and thus seriously degrading its cohesion and the fighting power that relied on it. There were still gaps in training and more importantly doctrine, but the US armoured force now had a bedrock of invaluable experience upon which to build.

ANALYSIS

The British in North Africa defeated the Italians in December 1940 because their force was entirely mobile. Their opponents were almost entirely infantry without transport, which remained in static and immobile positions that could be defeated in quick succession. Italian tanks were mostly light and mechanically unreliable, and the British guns outranged their artillery. Each Italian division had only two regiments and their positions lacked depth. Training and morale were low. Italian generals prioritized firepower over mobility and counterattacking. Communications were lacking and senior commanders did not know what was happening to their formations.

This decisive operation justified British confidence in their doctrine, and showed them that all they had to do was to place their tanks on the enemy's communication lines and decisive results would follow. Infantry did not have to cooperate with tanks and enemy tanks did not have to be targeted offensively by AT guns. Tanks could disperse and, in the desert, harass the enemy to persuade them they were against a much superior enemy. This would work only against an enemy with low morale. Artillery was dispersed to support these mobile columns.

The gains achieved in 1940 were lost when Rommel arrived in March 1941 with the DAK. The British were driven back to the Egyptian frontier. The plan in November in Operation *Crusader* was to eliminate the DAK's armour by luring them into a massive battle at Gabr Saleh; however, the British were happy to disperse their three armoured brigades, as they thought any of them was equal to a panzer division. Lieutenant-General Norrie had to eliminate the German and Italian armour; he also needed to guard the flank of the British infantry advancing nearer the sea. During Operation *Crusader* the three British armoured brigades were defeated in detail by Rommel's two panzer divisions.

The huge tank losses were explained by stating that German armour was superior and their crews experienced. Not until after *Crusader* did they realize that a lack of combined arms tactics was at fault. On 7 January 1942 Eighth Army HQ issued an edict stating that tanks must not move once in contact with the enemy unless artillery could cover them. The lessons learnt stated that tanks alone could not win battles and that they must operate in close cooperation with infantry and guns. The infantry tank also needed the close support of infantry and field guns because AT positions had destroyed the legend of their invincibility. A different approach was adopted whereby tanks would lure the enemy onto 25-pdr field guns deployed in the AT role. This dispersed the support that field artillery could provide to the infantry and there were not enough medium guns to compensate. A new decentralized theory of command based on the brigade as the main combined arms unit (to operate independently if

Montgomery standing beside an M3 Grant near Tripoli in Libya, 27 January 1943. Montgomery's approach to the use of his armoured forces was more conservative than that of Ritchie, and necessarily so, considering the parlous state of the force he inherited in the dog days of August. He took the time to rebuild morale and ensure that objectives were clearly understood, realistic and achievable. (Capt. Poston/Imperial War Museums via Getty Images)

A 2cm FlaK 38 set up in its air defence role early in the North African campaign, 24 March 1941. In a FlaK Abteilung the 2cm batteries were also used in the ground role, primarily to defend the heavy FlaK positions. With a rate of fire of 120rpm, it was fed by 20-round box magazines and used a 20×138mm B cartridge (including several AP variants). (Ullstein Bild via Getty Images)

necessary, in order to encourage them to command mixed armoured, motorized or lorried brigades) dispersed firepower even further.

The new approach was hindered by the lack of radios. In April 1941 Lieutenant-General Philip Neame, GOC Cyrenaica, had to rely on the Italian telephone system. The batteries of the radios belonging to 2nd Armoured Division could not be charged properly in 1941. In early 1942 armoured units were short of radio sets. Radio reception could be affected by geography; near Benghazi there was a spot where fading out was common. Atmospherics at night could make reception problematic. Ranges were inadequate. Most commanders could not operate radios themselves in order to listen in to what their subordinates were saying. The dispersal of armoured formations during the start of Operation *Crusader* was in part because of a signalling failure.

In May 1942 Ritchie deployed his infantry brigades in boxes along 80km of ground south of Gazala. They were not mutually supporting and had only mines to cover their flanks. Armour was kept in reserve to strike enemy armour that broke through. The British failed in that their armour was not concentrated in the correct position – they did not expect a southern approach. Infantry brigades were exposed to the DAK without tanks in support. The 3rd Indian Motor Brigade was defeated by German armour on 27 May, as were 7th Motor Brigade by 90.Leichte-Division, 4th Armoured Brigade by 15.Panzer-Division and 22nd Armoured Brigade by the two German panzer divisions. On 29 May, 2nd Armoured Division attacked two German panzer divisions and suffered heavy losses. On 30 May 1942, when 2nd and 22nd Armoured brigades attacked the Cauldron, they had no infantry to assault the AT guns. Artillery could not spot guns at the ranges German AT guns fired from. On 12–13 June tanks of 2nd, 4th and 22nd Armoured brigades charged Rommel's AT screen and suffered their worst defeat of the desert war.

The ability to manoeuvre to achieve force superiority and fight using combined arms achieved battlefield success in the desert. The British could fight using combined arms at a small unit level; however, hampered by their communications technology and doctrine, they had the tendency to disperse their forces. Their combined arms forces used in 1941 and 1942 were only able to raid German supply columns and were a nuisance to the Germans and little else. The 25-pdr guns were dispersed, and because of the lack of a larger-calibre AT gun were used as AT guns. The Germans were able to recover many of their tanks at night and repair them. The British would think they had destroyed them.

Tactical successes on both sides could not be made into operational victories because of the logistical limitations that existed, especially in the desert. In North Africa the distances involved needed large dumps. In December 1941, 2nd Armoured Division in Cyrenaica had no railhead close to its positions, and at 563km from the nearest base, did not have enough trucks to build a reserve. In March 1942 the railway from Mersa Matruh was extended to Capuzzo. Civilian trucks with lighter engines were used that were two-wheeled drive to carry supplies from the railhead to the front, about 64km. After El Alamein in October 1942 the incessant rains bogged down supply vehicles. The Germans had some of the same problems, as their army was based on the belief they would cover only short distances on terrain with good transport links. Their reach exceeded their logistical grasp.

German policy stressing AT guns should be used offensively against enemy tanks was proved correct. Kampfgruppen moved in combined arms formations and could use different components to support each other. Tanks, when encountering enemy tanks, would withdraw into AT positions that would ambush the enemy. German tanks would move around the enemy's flanks. Mobile command posts brought the German commanders closer to the front. They used ultra-low-frequency radios to monitor their own tanks' radios and did not have to wait for reports to reach them. Battle drills enabled formation commanders to operate without written orders and with short radio messages. This meant German leaders could better use their own initiative. Italian armoured and motorized formations from September 1941 were also effective. They opened a path to Rommel through minefields in the battle in the Cauldron in May 1942, saving the DAK.

The Americans would undergo many of the same lessons that the British had paid so dear to learn. They entered the Tunisian campaign with an outdated doctrine that had far too little to say about combined arms operations, tank fighting and dealing with AT weapons. It left their armour horribly vulnerable to the highly capable combined arms Kampfgruppen of the DAK and 10.Panzer-Division. Weaknesses in tank design were more readily blamed than doctrinal or cultural factors, but the battles in Tunisia did allow the Armored Force to develop a hard-won body of experience that would help inform changes to doctrine that would bear fruit in Sicily, Italy and Normandy.

AFTERMATH

For the first half of the war, British tank development was hamstrung by systemic problems of design and production, exacerbated by the infantry/cruiser doctrine. The understanding that a tank could find itself acting in support of infantry, bolstering defensive positions, exploiting a breakthrough, or engaging enemy tanks, eventually led to the development of the A-41 Centurion from 1943, though it was not fielded until days before the war's end. Perhaps more important was the development in doctrine.

After Operation *Crusader* each armoured brigade would have a field artillery regiment affiliated; however, the guns could not bring a sufficient volume of fire to neutralize enemy AT gun positions. The development of artillery in support of armour units by 1943 would enable the suppression of enemy AT defences. The 25-pdr did not have to target enemy armour because the 6-pdr was deployed to infantry battalions. The integration of infantry and guns into armour units commenced in Tunisia was practised further. The end of the campaign in Tunisia meant British armoured units could experience some rest. The 2nd Armoured Brigade was sent to Libya. By October they had moved to Boufarik in Algeria, where they practised indirect fire support to infantry. The brigade was in Italy in May 1944 where close support of infantry was the task assigned the unit. In August, 10th Hussars were given Shermans with 76mm guns and reassigned to operate against tanks. In September, 2nd Armoured Brigade's task was to break the Gothic Line.

Further developments in 8.8cm design made the gun a better AT weapon. The PaK-43, developed in 1943, would be lower and easier to hide. With no need to engage planes, the gun could present a low silhouette. It was issued to the Panzerjäger-Abteilungen of some armoured divisions and, where available, infantry divisions also, often as part of a mixed unit with PaK-40 guns as well.

The FlaK units serving with the DAK, Hermann Göring Division and 10.Panzer-Division were all lost at the end of the campaign in Tunisia, but their importance in AT operations was well established and would continue in the campaigns for Sicily, Italy and mainland Europe. FlaK units employed in the AT role could still be drawn from the Luftwaffe, but it was increasingly common for armoured divisions to have an integral Heeres-FlaK-Abteilung as part of their TO&E. The FlaK 41 remained primarily an air defence weapon, and saw no serious action as an AT gun.

A Crusader III tank in the foreground (with Crusader IIs in the background) advancing across Libya in pursuit of the retreating DAK, autumn/winter 1942. The main difference between the Crusader I and II and the Crusader III was the replacement of the 2-pdr (40mm) gun with the much more effective 6-pdr (57mm) gun. However, the size of the weapon meant that the turret became too cramped, reducing the crew to three from four (or even five if the Besa MG turret on the hull was in use) in the earlier models. There were 100 Crusader IIIs available for El Alamein. (Keystone/Getty Images)

BIBLIOGRAPHY

Calhoun, Mark T., *Defeat at Kasserine. American Armor Doctrine, Training, and Battle Command in Northwest Africa, World War II*, MA Thesis, US Army Command and General Staff College, Fort Leavenworth, KS (2003)

Dawnay, Brigadier D., *The 10th Royal Hussars in the Second World War 1939–1945*, Gale & Polden, Aldershot (1948)

Fennell, Jonathan, *Combat and Morale in the North African Campaign: The Eighth Army and the Path to El Alamein*, Cambridge University Press, Cambridge (2014)

——, *Fighting the People's War: The British and Commonwealth Armies and the Second World War*, Cambridge University Press, Cambridge (2019)

Fletcher, David, *The Great Tank Scandal: British Armour in the Second World War. Part 1*, HMSO, London (1989)

——, *British Battle Tanks: British-made tanks of WWII*, Osprey Publishing, Oxford (2017)

FM 17-10, *Armored Force Field Manual: Tactics and Techniques*, US War Department, US Government Printing Office, Washington, DC (1942)

Forty, George, *The Royal Tank Regiment: A Pictorial History 1916–1987*, Guild Publishing, London (1989)

French, David, *Raising Churchill's Army: The British Army and the War Against Germany 1919–1945*, OUP, Oxford (2001)

Gander, Terry, *German 88: The Most Famous Gun of the Second World War*, Pen & Sword Books, Barnsley (2012)

Howe, George F., *"Old Ironsides": The Battle History of the 1st Armored Division*, Battery Press, Nashville, TN (1979)

Jentz, Thomas L., *Tank Combat in North Africa: The Opening Rounds – Operations Sonnenblume, Brevity, Skorpion and Battle Axe*, Schiffer Publishing, Atglen, PA (1998)

——, *Dreaded Threat: The 8.8 cm Flak 18/36/37 in the Anti-Tank Role*, Panzer Tracts, Boyds, MD (2001)

Kurowski, Franz, *Das Afrika Korps: Erwin Rommel and the Germans in Africa, 1941–43*, Stackpole Books, Mechanicsburg, PA (2010)

Marwan-Schlosser, Rudolf F., *Rommels Flak als Pak: das Flak-Regiment 135 als Rückgrat des Deutschen Afrikakorps*, Weilburg Verlag, Wiener Neustadt (1991)

McNab, Chris, *Flak 88 Owner's Manual. 8.8cm Flugzeugabwehrkanone (Models 18/36/37/41)*, Haynes Publishing, Sparkford, Yeovil (2018)

Millen, Raymond A., *The Resilient Defense*, Paper No. 100, The Institute of Land Warfare. The Association of the United States Army, Arlington, VA (2014)

Moreman, Tim, *Desert Rats. British 8th Army in North Africa, 1941–43*, Osprey Publishing, Oxford (2007)

Müller, Werner, *Die 8.8cm FLAK 18-36-37-41 (2. Heft)*, Waffen-Arsenal 101. Podzun-Pallas-Verlag, Friedberg (1986)

——, *8.8cm Flak im Einsatz: Erster und Zweiter Weltkrieg*, Waffen-Arsenal 147, Podzun-Pallas-Verlag, Friedberg (1994)

Norris, John, *88 mm FlaK 18/36/37/41 & PaK 43, 1936–45*, New Vanguard 046, Osprey Publishing, Oxford (2002)

Piekalkiewicz, Janusz, *The German 88 Gun in Combat: The Scourge of Allied Armour*, Schiffer Publishing, Atglen, PA (1992)

Rottman, Gordon L., *M3 Medium Tank vs Panzer III, Kasserine Pass 1943*, Duel 010, Osprey Publishing, Oxford (2008)

Scheibert, Horst, *8,8 cm FLAK*, Waffen-Arsenal 027, Podzun-Pallas-Verlag, Friedberg (1976)

TM E9-369A, *German 88-mm Antiaircraft Gun Materiel*, War Dept, Washington, DC (1943)

TM 9-1904, *Ammunition Inspection Guide*, War Dept, Washington, DC (1944)

Trojca, Waldemar, *8,8 cm Flak 18-36-37 (1)*, Model Hobby, Katowice (2005)

Williamson, Gordon, *Knight's Cross and Oak-Leaves Recipients 1941–45*, Elite 123, Osprey Publishing, Oxford (2005)

Charging over rough Tunisian terrain, a US Army M4 seeks out German armoured units in the wake of other American tanks whose tread marks have scarred the soil, having recently helped rout Rommel's forces from the Bir Marbott Pass, Tunisia. The M4 would be the workhorse of Allied armoured formations until the end of the war, offering a good balance between armour, mobility and striking power. (Corbis via Getty Images)

INDEX

Figures in **bold** refer to illustrations.